CHRIST & DEMONS

UNSEEN REALMS OF DARKNESS

TRINITY ROYAL

Christ & Demons

Unseen Realms of Darkness
Trinity Royal

CONTENTS

Free books to our readers

War in Heaven came to Earth. Satan Rebellion:

https://dl.bookfunnel.com/ea12ys3dmk

Your Life in Heaven:

https://dl.bookfunnel.com/vg451qpuzs

Dedicated to my late Father who was a victim of evil spirits.

"The reason the Son of God appeared was to destroy the Devil's work." -Ephesians 6:12

INTRODUCTION

It is true that we are living in an age of massive and unparalleled scientific achievement today. Science, engineering, and technology have improved our lives massively, providing us with clean energy, bountiful food, and cures for many of the worst diseases that have bedeviled us since time immemorial. Yet, despite these accomplishments, it is not necessarily true that science alone has all the answers for absolutely everything human beings have ever encountered.

As Jamie Ballard noted in 2019, even in the modern-day United States, which has reached the highest level of economic and technological development on Earth, large proportions of the population still fervently believe in higher realities and spiritual entities, such as ghosts, demons, and other kinds of spirits. Nearly half, or 46%, believe that demons certainly or probably exist, and a similar proportion says the same thing about ghosts and other kinds of supernatural beings. More than a third believe they have directly felt the presence of at least one of these entities, and a little over a tenth think they have been affected by or been able to directly communicate with a ghost or spirit. Women are somewhat more likely than men to believe in these phenomena.

This book will tell you everything you need to know about these sorts of supernatural beings and many more, that you may not have even heard of before. We will start from the very beginning with the most basic and foundational concepts and move on to advanced teachings that will provide the knowledge you need to interact with spiritual entities on your terms, not theirs. The first chapters will define the phenomena of "Darkness" as well as what, specifically, makes demons and some spirits and ghosts "Dark." They will also explain what the Bible says about these Dark entities and what Christ taught about them and how to deal with them.

The middle chapters explain the mental and spiritual weapons used by demons and other evil spirits against human beings, as well as important methods to recognize attacks from the Darkness in order to protect yourself and help other people.

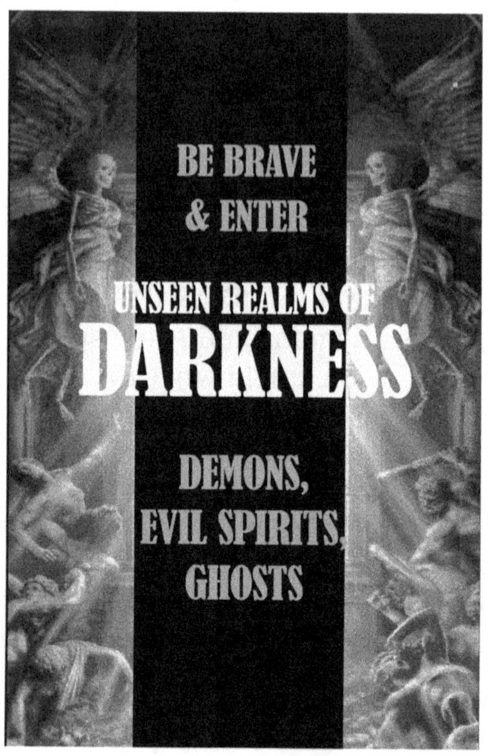

Finally, we will explain what will occur during Christ's Second Coming and how He will directly combat the evil spiritual entities that had previously been working in the shadows and conclude with an assessment of how progress and goodness can actually arise out of a struggle against the Dark.

Demons, Spirits, and the Dark Through Time and Space

Western countries are far from the only ones that have acknowledged the existence of spiritual entities, both beneficial and malicious. Virtually all cultures throughout history have, over time, created extensive and rich systems of categorization and analysis for supernatural creatures, whether they were called demons, devils, ghosts, goblins, evil nature spirits, or hybrid creatures.

The ancient Zoroastrians of Persia believed in "Daevas," whereas today, pious Jains believe in emissaries of hell called Narakas, and traditional Japanese religion has accounts of one, who are the attendants of the gods of the underworld. All of these traditions, and many others besides, think such evil entities are dedicated to hindering or harming humanity, preventing us from reaching a complete and positive relationship with God or higher spiritual realities. They're also believed to simply be keeping us from reaching our full potential as people or to be inflicting physical or mental harm on us by spreading disease, nightmares, or psychological maladies.

The focus of this book will be exclusively on these evil entities. It will not discuss spiritual beings of goodwill who serve Heaven and are aligned with the Light—thankfully, they certainly do exist as well, and indeed provide a great deal of assistance to humans in fighting off assaults from the Dark. However, to discuss them in the detail they deserve would be beyond the scope of the present work. This book will also rely primarily on the Bible as a starting point for discussion and analysis of spiritual realities—though anyone interested in the subject, regardless of background, will find it a valuable resource—and it will also incorporate recent secular studies and scholarship pertaining to the history and social science.

What the Bible Says

Demons feature prominently in many places in the Bible—the Good Book is abundantly clear that they exist, fight against God, and are relentlessly opposed to human flourishing. The First Epistle of John 3:8 explicitly states: "The one who does what is sinful is of the Devil because the Devil has been sinning from the beginning. The reason the Son of God appeared was to destroy the Devil's work." Ephesians 6:12 also states that "For our struggle is not against flesh and blood, but against the rulers, against the authorities, against the powers of this dark world and against the spiritual forces of evil in the heavenly realms." From these passages we can discern two things: That the Devil exists and Christ will lead us to battle against him, but also that the Devil is not a material being of "flesh and blood," but a spiritual one. The same applies to the many servants and saboteurs the Devil sends to our world to hinder our moral and spiritual progress and prevent Christ's will from being carried out—they are not creatures of flesh and blood but need to be detected and fought through non-physical means as well.

The fact that these entities are non-physical is why so many people do not believe in them, and it is also why even believers are caught in a constant, never-ending struggle with them. Though we cannot see them with our eyes, or even detect them with scientific technology, demons and the forces of Darkness are everywhere on Earth, reaching into the material realm from their hideouts in spiritual, nonmaterial realities so that they have reached their evil tendrils just about everywhere in our existence. So pervasive is their influence that in a way, evil and darkness are fully integrated into our lives, so much so that it can be difficult to distinguish them from what is not.

Darkness, Light, and Christ

The duality of the entire universe–not just planet Earth, but all of the solar systems in all of the galaxies, as well as higher dimensions—is between light and darkness. We can also define these terms as virtue and vice, or good and evil. In Heaven, all is light, or goodness. Altruism, charity, honesty, and every other form of positive and pro-social thought and behavior are the only things that exist. By contrast, and as you can expect, in Hell, the opposite obtains–selfishness and cruelty provide what passes for order in that realm. Our world of Earth, rather than belonging entirely to those two extremes, is a site of constant conflict between them. There are wars, thefts, and other crimes we see around us all the time, but also many good people displaying valor, kindness, and heroism as well. Earth would indeed look just like Heaven if there was no evil present on it, but as mentioned above, the constant efforts of the Devil and his supernatural servants have infested the fabric of our reality itself with darkness, making it almost impossible to overcome.

Almost impossible, however, not entirely impossible. There is indeed hope for all of us ordinary human beings to triumph over the limitless and cunning forces of evil: Jesus Christ. Indeed, one of the primary reasons He came to Earth in the first place, over two thousand years ago, was to fight the Devil and his servants and give the human race a chance for ultimate salvation. Even following His original ministry, crucifixion, and resurrection, however, Christ did not complete everything necessary for the final triumph of Light over Dark, and there are still several elements of His agenda that are currently incomplete. This is why Christ did not just leave us to our own devices, which would also leave us entirely vulnerable to a counterattack from the Devil, but promised to return someday far in the future, which we know as the Second Coming, as written in Matthew 24:30: "Then will appear the sign of the Son of Man in Heaven. And then all the peoples of the earth will mourn when they see the Son of Man coming on the clouds of Heaven, with power and great glory." We will describe the events of the Second Coming and its final results in a later chapter. For now, just keep in mind that all the various Dark entities and the weapons used by these entities you will read about over the course of this book, have always been arrayed against Jesus Christ, and He is the One most able to defeat them. Indeed, the primary purpose of the Second Coming is to defeat the Darkness once and for all!

Appeals and Risks of Studying the Supernatural

As you have probably gathered by this point, the supernatural is a very weighty subject. As Tendai Kashiri (2023) has noted, spiritual realities, which rely on insight not even technology can provide, are considered by some people to be even more intriguing than science and engineering, despite the aforementioned immense accomplishments of those fields of study. This is precise because spiritual matters are harder to grasp and also perceived to be equally or more important because their influence is felt across all of human history, not just the modern age, and because of what they imply about our ultimate destiny and our fates after death, which not even science has been able to penetrate.

In addition to these sociological factors, there are three psychological ones that make the supernatural so compelling for human beings. The first is the general allure of the unknown. Humans are naturally curious creatures, driven to know everything we can about the world around us, and if we can't find an easy answer to a question, we very easily drive ourselves to distraction trying to figure out what such an answer could be. Since the supernatural has seemed so prevalent in our experience, yet so resistant to the explanations of science and engineering, it represents a great, unknown vista that is irresistible to our psyches.

Second is the way the supernatural symbolizes our own internal struggles. Though obviously not as dramatic as Christ's contest with the Devil on the mountain, every human being deals with a conflict between Light and Darkness in their own personal lives. We all struggle with moral choices: To be kind rather than cruel, honest rather than deceitful, and so on. Sometimes we win these internal struggles, and sometimes we lose, with the results playing out in our own lives and how we relate to the people around us. And since the larger spiritual conflict between Light and Dark is a macrocosm of our internal ones, we are driven to learn more about the supernatural entities involved in the greater war, to gain a better perspective on our own.

Finally, human beings want an external explanation for the presence of evil and suffering in the world. Though some things like warfare can be partially attributed to human choices, there seems to be so much senseless suffering in the world, ranging from acts of extreme cruelty to the terrors of nature such as disasters and disease, that many people find it more comforting (or at least less absurd) to blame it on powerful entities which can also think for themselves, who wish ill on humans and want to see us suffer. That makes seemingly chaotic events easier to understand, given how many people find a truly mindless, indifferent universe even more frightening than a malicious one. Thus, they postulate the existence of malicious supernatural creatures.

As fascinating as the topic of the supernatural can be, by now you have probably figured out that it can indeed be very dangerous for people who pursue it haphazardly or half-heartedly. The Bible is crystal clear about how powerful the Devil and his servants are, with its many descriptions of them causing chaos in human affairs, as well as the dire fate awaiting those who willingly consort with or give themselves over to the forces of Darkness. But even if you are a good-hearted person, an innocent interest in the supernatural without the proper respect for it can allow malicious demons or spirits to gradually work their way into your psyche, slowly but surely twisting your soul, or in some cases, a lack of caution can even lead to direct spiritual (and occasionally physical!) assault by these entities. This book is intended to explain why these evil beings seek to do us harm, discuss what roles they ultimately play in Christ's plans, and provide some guidance on how we can support Christ and protect ourselves from His foes, but it is absolutely not an extensive instruction manual for communicating with, much less influencing, spiritual entities. Spiritual warfare is not to be taken lightly and should certainly not be pursued by beginners, so readers of this text should definitely defer to wisdom and prudence, and refrain from seeking out contact with supernatural entities even if such entities might appear at first to be friendly.

Lucifer Rebellion - How Evil got to Planet Earth

If there was no evil on planet Earth, it would have been a Heavenly realm also. Since we are not in Heaven at the moment, so what happened?

The difference between Heaven and not-so-Heaven is the presence of darkness or duality of good and bad, God like and not-so God like, in other words presence of those that follow God and those that do not follow God.

So how did darkness come to planet Earth?

The answer is Lucifer Rebellion. There was a great War in Heaven that devastated the Universe for thousands of years and this War found its way to planet Earth. This is the single most important event in the history of the Universe. Also, this is the only event worth talking about that shaped the history of planet Earth. Every other event on Earth or Heavens bar none dwarfs in comparison.

This great war, Lucifer Rebellion is mentioned only twice in our Holy scriptures, yet without this War in Heaven and its impact on Earth, there is absolutely no reason for Christ to come to planet Earth. I have discussed this War in Heaven extensively in my other book titled -Lucifer Rebellion. Christ vs Satan – Final Battle for Earth has Begun".

In this single chapter, let's look at a summary.

War in Heaven

All the major religions of the world including Christianity, Islam, Judaism, Hinduism, and Buddhism agree on one critical fact – there is Heaven and hell, God and His adversary, and Light and Dark, and both are opposites. The adversary is called by different names including Satan, Shaitan, Iblis, and Lucifer. All religions also agree both factions are powerful adversaries and that Human beings are somehow part of this epic battle. Most of the details in all of the scriptural texts are either high-level or sketchy at best, there is no explanation. This is subject to different interpretations and confusion among theologians.

The Holy Bible when seen through the lens of history has more info comparatively than most other religious scriptures about the war in heaven but this also falls short.

Lucifer Rebellion and the Fall of the Devil

God Created Lucifer as a unique being in that he was an Angel, the most beautiful angel of all created, and he had free will, and the ability to make his own decisions and act on them. The original Aramaic name Lucifer translates to Morning Star. Lucifer is mentioned in the Bible only two times but is said to have sat at God's side and worshiped him and loved him deeply. Lucifer was regarded as the wisest, greatest, and most beautiful angel in all of the creation. He is described as the most beautiful and brightest angel in existence and regarded as the perfection of beauty and wisdom. His beauty exceeded all other angels in heaven to the point where a mere glance would make anyone go mad from sheer beauty and power. He is noted to have six colossal whitish gold wings, that almost looked made of light. According to the old testament, when Lucifer was in heaven his clothing was adorned with many precious stones all beautifully crafted for him and set in the finest gold.

Due to Lucifer being the favored creation, God would reveal to him, His plans for the creation. The more God told Lucifer His plans; the more problems Lucifer began to see in God's plan. His thoughts began to stray from what his Father desired. Eventually, it led to a series of heated arguments between God and Lucifer. Lucifer's paranoia made him see God as a tyrannical ruler and declared that he had a better plan for the universe and that he would exalt his throne above God. Lucifer finally launched his "Declaration of Liberty".

> "I will ascend into heaven, I will exalt my throne above the stars of God; I will also sit on the mount of the congregation on the farthest sides of the north; I will also ascend the heights of the clouds, I will be like the Most High." – Isaiah 14:13-14

He proposed a new Creation concept. Lucifer sincerely believed that with his new creation, he could enhance and fasten spiritual growth compared to the current process of step-by-step evolution under God's rule. Lucifer wanted to be the creator of souls, he thought that by using laboratory methods, machine intelligence, and his creative abilities, he is able to give a portion of himself to create new souls that can evolve faster with higher intelligence, that the current way under Gods ruling which is a slow, long and methodical process of evolution.

Additionally, Lucifer also proposed the concept of "karma", which is cause and effect. What you sow you reap. He sincerely believed that this will help the souls to learn and evolve faster. As talented and charming as he is, he was able to sell his concept of new creation and evolution to 1/3rd of the angels in heaven.

With 1/3rd of the angels, Lucifer waged a full-fledged war against God.

"And there was war in heaven: Michael and his angels fought against the dragon, and the dragon fought and his angels, And prevailed not; neither was their place found anymore in heaven. And the great dragon was cast out, that old serpent, called the Devil, and Satan, which deceiveth the whole world: he was cast out into the earth, and his angels were cast out with him." - [Revelation 12:7-9]

Christ defeated Lucifer and then banished him and his followers from Heaven. And so did Lucifer Fall from grace with the utmost tragedy, horror, dismay, and terror.

He was cast to the Earth, and his angels were cast out with him. – Revelations 12:9

"And I beheld Satan fall as lightning from heaven." - Luke 10:18

The Book of Isaiah also records this event -

"How you are fallen from heaven, O Lucifer, son of the morning! How you are cut down to the ground, you who weakened the nations! For you have said in your heart: 'I will ascend into heaven, I will exalt my throne above the stars of God; I will also sit on the mount of the congregation on the farthest sides of the north; I will ascend above the heights of the clouds, I will be like the Most High'" (Isaiah 14:12-14).

Devil

The devil has many titles in the Bible, such as Satan, Lucifer, Beelzebub, and others. The word Satan means "the adversary", the devil means "the accuser", and Lucifer which is used only two times in the Bible is translated as "star of the morning". The Bible uses these titles interchangeably, such as in Revelation 20:2 which says "He seized the dragon, the ancient serpent, who is the devil, or Satan, and bound him for a thousand years." Throughout the scriptures, it is clear that all of these titles refer to an entity that is opposed to God, and is identified by his attributes, "accuser", "adversary", and so on. In short, Satan or Lucifer is a fallen angel, but this necessitates further explanation.

Note: Lucifer and Satan or Devil names are used interchangeably in this book. Since the ideology is the same, the names are interchangeable.

After the Fall

After the Fall, Lucifer and his cohorts gradually expanded their control over this section of our universe. About 200,000 years ago the rebellion entered our section of the galaxy and then Earth. Many leaders of the different planets of this universe were either captured or taken over cleverly by Lucifer. Leaders and planetary princes (a planetary prince can be likened to the president/prime minister of the planet) of more than 700 planets in our local universe bowed to Lucifer.

God and Christ saw that things were not going well for the Universe and decided to localize the battle. This served two purposes. First to attract all darkness to the identified world(s), so the effects can be localized and the dark army's fate can be determined once and for all; secondly, the localization can prevent further dark infestation to other galaxies and other parts of the universe.

Fall of Earth to Lucifer Rebellion

"Spiritual warfare is very real. There's a furious, fierce, and ferocious battle raging in the realm of the spirit between the forces of God and the forces of evil. Warfare happens every day, all the time. Whether you believe it or not, you are

on a battlefield. You are in warfare." — Pedro
Okoro

In the grand constellation picture, planet Earth is one of
the unique shining "Pearl" created by Christ with the help
of God. The illumination of the crystal blueish color is
extremely eye-catching and glittering among the shining
stars in the local universe. Earth attracted many space
travelers to check out and set foot on the surface. Some
of them were involved to set up their settlements when
their "Home" planets were in "trouble". All their needs and
wants were fully met and supplied without conditions.
Their descendants were living without worry and with
full compassion and love, walking freely with abundance
while learning their lessons and experiences. All lived a
high nobility life and worked toward their soul evolutionary
journey.

The planetary prince of Earth at that time is Caligastia. Satan successfully swayed him to join his rebellion. They established headquarters in Mesopotamia. This is the beginning of the fall of Earth. Satan successfully breached the barrier between Hell and Earth, this signaled the beginning of the Apocalypse.

For two hundred millennia, the battle continued in this part of the local galaxy until it centered on our world, planet Earth.

Note: The above is a short summary of the War in Heaven, the reality of Lucifer/Satan/Devil, and how the Fall happened. If you want a thorough and detailed understanding, please check out my book "Christ vs Satan – Final Battle for Earth has Begun", which is part of "The

Real Matrix Series". Will have a link at the end of this book if interested.

Purpose of the War – For your Soul

Now that the Earth is under the control and influence of Dark Lords, it has become a challenge for Humanity to grow spiritually and become closer to God. So, God sends numerous beings over many centuries to advance the cause of Light. But what exactly do these beings of Light teach? All great teachers taught us how to grow in consciousness and become closer to God. Soul evolution. It is your soul that both Darkness and Light are after. Both Light and Dark are fighting for control of your soul, the planet, and the humans on it. This single planet can change the course of the entire war for either side.

How the War is Fought

You're surely familiar with warfare from just watching the news. Whether it's the conflict in Ukraine as of the time of this writing, the Gulf War back in the 1990s, or the Vietnam War even earlier, you're probably familiar with the sound of gunfire, explosions, cannons, and missiles from jet planes flying overhead. But even those wars, as brutal as they were, had some rules attached to them. For instance, even though American and Soviet-backed countries fought constantly during the Cold War, neither the US nor the USSR used nuclear weapons against each other directly.

The spiritual conflict between Light and Dark is a total war in the truest sense, occurring over thousands of years and on many different planes of existence. But it, too, has rules, and you must be aware of those rules to make the right choices during the conflict.

The first rule is non-interference, at least directly. Satan and his angels will not physically manifest on earth and do battle with weapons like swords and guns, and neither will the forces of Light. Combat, for now, is mostly in unseen spiritual realms, as both sides try to gain influence over particular human beings who can shape human society as a whole in ways more amenable to one side or another. However, humans can petition either side for certain types of help if they ask directly.

Humans have the freedom to contact and follow either God or Devil. Free will is the greatest gift of our creator. Some humans contact Lucifer's agents to gain knowledge of dark arts like using spells to cloud people's minds or gain social or political influence or summon demonic entities from other realms, etc. Contacting beings of Light can offer more positive effects, both personally—providing better mental health and a sense of well-being—and on a larger scale, by soothing people's minds to make them more peaceful or appealing to their better natures to give rise to positive social programs or matters like that.

The vast majority of human beings on earth are unaware of this spiritual conflict. And even those who are aware of it, like you are now, cannot see everything going on in the great Light-Dark war. While you may be able to recollect some wisdom from them under very particular circumstances, and while the virtue you display in this life has some impact, you lose virtually all of your concrete memories when you pass away. That is precisely why you should try to do the best you can in this lifetime. You must rely on yourself to navigate the time you spend on earth that you're aware of. The wisdom contained in this book can help you on your path to advancement. The Universal Father's mercy is boundless, and he wants everyone to reach him eventually, no matter how long it takes or how much difficulty they might have.

The one exception to these rules can be found in our DNA. Living in the modern world, you're probably aware of how DNA is the building block of life, the blueprints according to which our cells grow and develop, and thus the foundation of our physical bodies. However, DNA contains traces of spiritual truth as well. With special training, you can access buried memories within your DNA. It can be very hard to get full memories, so most of the time, you can only access fragments, but once you know of the existence of the spiritual matrix, and higher realms of consciousness to which you can ascend, your soul journey can be enlightening.

Some of these memories in your DNA contain 'codes' for not only moral virtue and heroism in our universe, but the secrets of enlightenment and advancement towards the higher planes. This knowledge is supernatural in the truest sense—even if you had not experienced it so far, the Universal Father and his angels spread it throughout the fabric of the universe, where it became attached to certain strands of DNA. This supernatural genetic knowledge is crucial to future battles in the great war. We know there have been many battles on Earth related to suppressing the lighted DNA. The DNA wars are real. It is beyond the scope of this book to discuss these topics.

Perhaps if humanity manages to shake off the influence of the Dark entirely, the veil separating Humans and Angels can be lifted, but until then, we must wage our struggle quarantined from the rest of the universe. Yet another reason the present battle on earth is so important; either Light or Dark will win, and the prize they are after is your soul. You, as an individual, can influence how the entire universe will turn out!

The Prize: Your Soul

Lucifer does not want our bodies in and of themselves, but our minds—our souls—generate energy that his forces desperately need. The darkness feeds off negative emotional energies from humans. This makes Dark beings strong. The stronger they are, the more darkness they hold. Higher Dark entities can effortlessly subjugate a normal human being. Once you are subjugated and controlled, you become a weapon of Darkness. You are mind-controlled.

Souls are eternal and pass through time by gaining different experiences. Death of the human physical body is not the end for en-souled beings that can think. Now, the activity of the soul—that which directs us towards good, virtuous deeds (producing illuminated, holy souls) or evil ones (producing tainted, condemned souls)— creates spiritual echoes across the universe and all of creation, including the higher universes from which Lucifer originally came, reaching all the way to Paradise. At least, that is the case most of the time. However, the actions of souls, mediated through the physical shells they currently occupy, can be good or bad. This energy is used by either side to further the agenda.

Many creatures from all across many universes can provide spiritual energy in this way. But humans on earth, due to the intensity of our emotional being and the capacity to generate intense amounts of energy based on belief patterns and our actions and our lives.

Therein lies the heart of Satan's plan. Satan plans to turn Earth into a gigantic prison of shadows. There, human beings will be enslaved and trapped, our souls no longer able to advance to higher universes. Our souls will be imprisoned on earth, where they will be used to fuel Lucifer and his fallen angels in their dark crusade against the Universal Father and his loyal ones. Satan needs human souls to further their agenda and cannot just annihilate us.

Light, by contrast, does not want to trap souls for selfish use—quite the opposite. The forces of Light want Earth and its human populations to evolve rather than stagnate and languish in prison. When human beings express virtue and thus ascend to higher universes or worlds on higher vibratory levels (to use technical terms), their souls emit light energy which strengthens God's forces on Earth to help free more souls and further the co-creation process. This is good for both individuals and the universe as a whole, and the souls who, have ascended to the highest vibratory level of all (Paradise) are true juggernauts in the struggle against darkness.

Thus, both sides have a very vested interest in you. Yes, you, the person reading this book right now! Your actions here and now, in this world, and the beliefs you hold, not only influence your life but the lives of others, by extension. This will ultimately influence the course of the final battle between Light and Dark–which side will your soul's energy go to? You must make the right decision.

What is a Soul and how does it Evolve?

I have discussed this topic in great detail in other books. The following is an extract from one of the chapters in the book – SOS-Save yOur Soul.

1. **What does being alive actually mean? What is Spirit?**

God's spark resides with-in each of us. This divine spark of life is Sprit with-in. This is God's breath of life. This gives our material body "life". You and I are in the image of God. Each of us has a direct connection to God as God's spirit is within us.

2. What are the un-seen constituents that make each one of us?

The first un-seen part of us is the Spirit with-in (God's divine spark of life) that gives us the breath of life. The second un-seen part of us is the Soul.

3. What exactly is Soul? When does it get birthed? How does it grow?

A soul is a construct that is born between ages four and five when the material mind starts to mature and develops will and reasoning ability. The soul resides in the material mind. The Mother of the Soul is Material-mind; Father of Soul is the Spirit with-in. So the soul is both material and non-material at the same time. Soul is semi-material in nature. It has some substance to it. The parents of soul are material-mind (which is material) and Spirit with-in (which is non-material).

Soul can choose to be materialistic (like its Mother material mind) or be non-materialistic (like the Divine Spirit within). This is souls choice that will ultimately determine if it will have eternal life or not.

4. What makes each of us unique? What is that which gives us a personality and identity?

All of our experiences are stored in our Soul. All our successes, failures, good and bad experiences are stored permanently in our soul. Our experiences make us who we are and also give us a unique personality. The spirit with-in gives us our identity. This identity come from God. God, Christ and Heavenly beings recognize us with our identity. This is similar to name that we give ourself in material world. There is only one like you in this creation. Your identity is unique and is your God's gift.

Until you truly know your spiritual nature and your connection with the Divine, life will continue to be a mystery. We are here today and gone tomorrow. When one passes over to the other side after death-sleep, this whole material world will soon become a dream. You do not grieve when you must change into a worn-out coat that has served its purpose. How foolish it is to think that this body (materialistic one) is permanent. It seems real now but will disappear.

The Primary Reason for Christ First Coming – Fight the Devil

I n a universe as vast as ours, with all of its solar systems and galaxies, why would the Divine take such an interest in a small planet orbiting an unremarkable star at the very edge of the Milky Way?

The Order of the Universe

The Bible is certainly one of the greatest books ever written. Christians obviously find it holy, but even members of other faiths, or no faith at all, can acknowledge the power of its moral teachings and the insight it provides into transcendent reality.

As the Bible teaches, there is only one supreme God, creator of humanity, Earth itself, and the heavens above, all the stars we see in the night sky, and many more beyond. So great is God's power that he did not create a single planet, but many thousands upon thousands—so very many that human beings can scarcely conceive of such a humongous multitude. In His infinite wisdom, in order to best minister to the innumerable beings who need His guidance, God will sometimes distribute His power in the form of spiritual servants to directly oversee galaxies, then solar systems, and then individual planets with life on them.

However, while the Bible concentrates primarily on God's interactions with human beings on Earth, we are not the only ones He is concerned with. By separating Himself into emissaries, and having those divine emissaries struggle through the responsibilities of overseeing galaxies, and planets, and occasionally even incarnating themselves physically to live amongst the mortals they rule, God shares the joy and pain of His creations, and thus the glory of their self-improvement as well, which does not contradict but enhances and deepens the already-existing glory of His divine nature, personality, and mode of existence.

Needless to say, it is very easy to understand how all of this would apply to Christ's appearance on Earth. God and His emissaries, being wise and caring, know they have to incarnate within a world in a material universe at precisely the right time and place, and in precisely the right social context (given the individual development of that world in terms of culture, religion and understanding of God and morality, socioeconomic factors, and so on) in order to leave the most positive impact.

For Earth, that time was 0 A.D., in the context of the Jewish people living under Roman rule in the Middle East. As the analysis of the Old Testament, we have performed earlier illustrates, the prophets and sages of Jewish history had made great strides in understanding God's will, His greatness, and the moral tenets He wanted His creations to uphold. Although cloaked in myth and allegory appropriate for a species that had not yet, at the time, created advanced science, Jewish teaching affirmed the omnibenevolence, uniqueness, and oneness of the Universal Father. The Old Testament also contained many powerful moral messages to ensure its adherents stayed on the right path: admonitions to protect orphans and widows, care for the poor, be honest and forthright in your dealings with everyone (even your enemies), and how God's mercy would always be extended to anyone who asked for it (NIV, Exodus 22:22-27).

The Backdrop of Earth Prior to Christ's First Coming

To really understand Christ's mission on this blue orb, we need to spend little time on why Christ decided to come to Earth. While there are many ways this can be interpreted, the primary reasons being:

- *to fight the devil*

- *Pave the way for Human salvation*

- *To teach Humans and establish communion with God the Father within.*

Prior to the birth of Christ, God's own Son, people had started to lose sight of God's teachings. Evil had an upper hand on Earth and planet affairs. To bring the people back to the most important basics (so to speak). The Universal Father's Son Christ (also known as Christ Michael in the higher levels of the Universe) decided to incarnate on planet Earth.

You might also be wondering: Why Earth, specifically? After all, given how vast our universe is, even if its creator, there are many millions of worlds in our universe. Why did He not incarnate (or, as the technical language goes, proceed through a Bestowal) on one of those? The answer has to do with what makes human beings particularly important in the grand scheme of things.

Darkness is concentrated on Earth – What happens on Earth has ripple effects across the Universe.

As we have seen before the dark forces have been quarantined to this sector of the galaxy, with Earth being the epicenter. Planet Earth is quarantined or locked down to arrest the spread of the virus of darkness.

In higher realms, planet Earth is called "The Planet of Sorrows" or "Earth Shawn". People on this planet suffer the most. If darkness is defeated here on Earth, it is certain to be defeated and eradicated in the rest of the universe where darkness exists.

If Christ has to save His own created Universe, the best place to target is the epicenter of evil, Planet Earth.

Earth is a seed planet – A very important one

There are usually very few (probably only one or two planets in the Galaxy or the local sector of the universe) planets deemed worthy of new Soul creation. When a planet is created, all life forms are in group consciousness. In due time with training and opportunities, the life-form takes on a unique identity. When this life-form is able to make its own choices or have a "will" of its own, it then begins to form mind packets of information which evolves into what we call the "Soul". Planet Earth is imbued with this unique God-given ability and so has a special place in the universe

To Free Human Souls from the Prison of Darkness

Now that the Earth is under the control and influence of Dark Lords, it has become a challenge for Humanity to grow spiritually and become closer to God. So God sends numerous beings over many centuries to advance the cause of Light. But what exactly do these beings of Light teach? All great teachers taught us how to grow in consciousness and become closer to God. How to evolve one's Soul to get closer to the heavenly Father.

It is your soul that both Darkness and Light are after. Both Light and Dark are fighting for control of your soul, and hence the planet. This single planet can change the course of the entire war for either side. Both God and Satan has a vested interest in your Soul.

Power of Human Emotions

Living in the modern world, everyone is familiar with power, defined in the broadest scientific sense as simply "the ability to do work." Steam power allows us to move great machines by boiling water, while nuclear power uses the energy generated by splitting atoms to do the same, or generate electricity and warmth, and so on. However, what many people are not aware of is that there is also spiritual power.

God the Father is the absolute height of spiritual power. Every sapient being in the entire universe possesses spiritual power as well. Sapience, or the ability to reason, think, and act morally, is much more than just a mundane material interaction of electrochemical stimuli. We human beings, and all the other thinking creatures on other planets, are far more than mere organic computers. Our acts of reasoning, as well as our demonstrations of benevolence, compassion, and obedience to God's laws, reflect the deeper layers of reality and thus influence those deeper layers. In other words, the experiences of thinking creatures in the material world can generate not only physical power but spiritual power as well.

Now, everyone knows that there are very many differentiations in the amount of physical power various systems generate. A steam engine, despite being very powerful and top of the line in the eighteenth century, does not generate as much power as a coal plant, and even those are less efficient and powerful (and worse for the environment barring catastrophes, to boot) than the most modern nuclear power plants, with fusion technology promising to generate even more. The same applies to spiritual power. For a variety of reasons too complex to describe in depth, human beings, out of all the beings in the universe, produce the highest amount of spiritual power per capita over the course of our lifetimes. Our emotions are so strong, the struggles we endure (and overcome) so grave, that our souls (those spiritual and mental parts that distinguish sapient material beings from mere animals) leave larger ripples in the etheric and astral levels of this universe than those of worlds elsewhere in the universe.

This spiritual power can be harnessed toward a multitude of different ends. The forces of Light, following the will of the Universal Father, would use it for good. God's desire for humans, as well as all mortal beings, is that they do good work over the course of their mortal lifespans, enhancing the positivity and purging the negativity in their souls. Death is not the end for sapient, soulful beings. In the ordinary course of things, if we have lived good lives and pursued wisdom and Godliness after we die, our mortal bodies may be gone but our souls remain, ascending towards higher spiritual levels, drawing closer to the Universal Father. As long as we uphold virtue and obey God's teaching, every life we pass brings us closer and closer to our ultimate goal of full communion with God. And this process, the ascendance of souls, produces a huge amount of spiritual power, with the ascendance of human souls producing the very highest amount possible in this universe.

Such positive "light" energy, in spiritual terms, allows higher spiritual beings to carry out their will—to perform more actions across a further span of time and space and within a shorter period of time. Thus can they generate more worlds, spend more time guiding and uplifting the residents of already existing worlds, refine the evolutionary processes of the worlds under their oversight, and so on.

Obviously, this process requires us to have a good grasp of morality and spiritual issues. And who better to teach us about them than a divine being Himself? Thus, Christ chose exactly the right time and place to restore the truths ancient Jews had previously discovered, incorporate them into even higher teachings, and spread them throughout the Roman empire, where they would remain established across the world. For the peoples of Earth, this would help them live better lives and ascend more easily to higher levels, and for the rest of the universe, would thus provide more spiritual energy for higher beings to perform good works. A win-win situation indeed!

Christ Bestowal on Planet Earth

Planet Earth is absolutely central to the battle between Light and Dark due to the comparatively massive amount of spiritual energy human beings produce. And while the struggle was slow, Lucifer was slowly but surely gaining the upper hand through a variety of means. His agents surreptitiously eliminated Light bloodlines on Earth, subverted the noble teachings of many great philosophers like Aristotle or Zoroaster, and placed merciless conquerors in positions of power (across the Roman empire, for instance) to keep humanity mired in war and oppression, preventing many of us from growing closer to God and moving to Heavens after death-sleep. It was getting harder and harder for agents of Light to access the planet, very few people could commune with the Universal Father at all, and the Dark had succeeded in turning many unfortunate human souls into perpetual energy batteries, fueling the campaign against God. These troubling developments drew the attention of not just God but the highest of His angels who had been charged with overseeing our universe.

This process became harder on Earth due to the spiritual isolation or quarantine Earth is subjected to. On the other hand, the forces of Light absolutely could not allow Earth to fall into the Dark, or else everything would be lost. Thus, Christ embarked upon the riskiest and most dangerous plan imaginable for an angel of his stature. He would undergo Bestowal and use all of his energies to penetrate the Matrix. However, due to the extreme cost of that procedure, Christ would appear on Earth not as a full-grown adult, but as a humble child, profoundly vulnerable to the many Dark forces seeking his destruction!

This was essentially Christ first coming. This was a completely secret mission between God and Christ, and not even the angles and arch angels in Paradise were aware. Only after His birth as a helpless small baby, the announcement went out to the entire headquarters of the universe in heavenly realms. Many were surprised as He did not bestow with powers intact but as a helpless babe. And yes, the baby is subjected to all rules of limited consciousness of the war-torn planet.

While there are many ways the first-coming mission can be interpreted, the primary purpose is to help light win the war and pave the way for Human salvation.

For Christ, the rewards were worth the risks. If he managed to grow to adulthood on Earth, this Bestowal would prove for all time that he was truly a gifted creator and administrator and that he deserved to be sovereign over his universe for all eternity. And not only that, but success in this mission would pave the way for Light's victory, as it would undo much of the progress Dark had made in subverting human society and turning people into Dark batteries. Indeed, such a triumph would liberate not only Earth, but also several nearby star systems whose inhabitants were not as important–in terms of energy generated–as humans, but who had nevertheless been conquered by Darkness. This would lead to a cascade effect, where the Devil's forces would subsequently grow weaker day after day, and the forces of Light grow stronger at the same rate, allowing a swift end to the entire Rebellion after the final battle on Earth. So incredibly important was this operation that it was kept secret from even the other angels. No one knew what God and Christ were planning until he had arrived— or more accurately, been born—on Earth!

CHRIST AND DEMONS IN THE BIBLE

As the Bible accounts, Christ demonstrated His power and authority in our world in a wide variety of ways. He cured diseases like leprosy, raised a woman's son from the dead (Luke 5:12, 14-15), and generally performed lots of heroic and miraculous acts that proved He was not just an ordinary man. Some of His most important activities, however, involved protecting humanity from supernatural, external threats, not just natural instances of death or disease. In this chapter, we will explore Christ's teachings about these external threats, prayers and states of mind that can protect us from such threats, and seven specific examples from the Bible where Christ dealt directly with evil spiritual agents of the Dark.

Evil in the Old Testament

From the very beginning of His public ministry among the peoples of the Roman-occupied Middle East, Jesus proclaimed that He was serving God and fulfilling the Lord's commands on Earth: "The time is fulfilled, and the Kingdom of God is at hand, repent and believe in the gospel" (Mark 1:14-15). In order to build up the Kingdom of God, it is necessary for His servants to understand who opposes them, why they will face such opposition, and what they should do about it.

The primary enemy of God's Kingdom, and by extension human health, progress, flourishing, and happiness, is the evil lord of Darkness and the commander of all lower Dark-aligned entities: Satan.

Even in the Old Testament, written millennia before Christ came to earth, there were descriptions and warnings of the threats he posed to man. In the allegory of the Garden of Eden, Adam and Eve are tossed out of what represents God's Kingdom, because they were misled by a "serpent" who offered them fruit from the tree of knowledge (Genesis 3:1-14). Again, since these passages are an allegory, we must understand that they refer to not a natural, normal snake or viper, but instead stand in for the more abstract concept of a spiritual force that seeks to mislead us and take us away from God, even through the most underhanded or seemingly circuitous means. This spiritual force is Satan, and the story of the Garden explains, albeit indirectly, how he managed to insert Darkness into the fabric of mundane human reality here on Earth, and if he was not so successful with that dastardly plan, humans would have to deal with many fewer temptations, it would be much easier for us to see God's providence in our lives, and so on.

The clearest example of Satan's activity in the Old Testament is in the Book of Job, where he sends down innumerable plagues and calamities upon God's most pious, devoted, and upright servant, Job, in order to "prove" (or try to prove) that Job's faith was just a sham, and that Job would reject God when he no longer had God's blessings. Thankfully, as the story goes, Job held on to his faith, and in the end, his maladies were cured and he was rewarded by God. But this story illustrates several things. First, that Satan and—as it was—his lesser servants try to work by appealing to human greed, spitefulness, and self-concern to separate us from God. Their reasoning is that our relationship with the Almighty is purely transactional, and if we encounter hardship that God can't immediately help with, we will lose our faith in Him. Don't let Satan be proven right: Even when times are difficult, keep in mind that God has a plan, and always keep praising Him and following His teachings, which will keep the Devil and his imps from worming their way into your mind and taking it over for Darkness.

Christ's Teachings Concerning Evil

Christ, as a pious and knowledgeable Jewish preacher, was already well aware of what the Old Testament taught about Satan, and He would reinforce those messages to His audience in Galilee and elsewhere. Consider the famous parable of the farmer and the seed. It is Satan who snatches away the kingdom seed before it can take root in a hearer's life (Mark 4:15). Here, Jesus is referring to Satan's propensity to sow doubts and dissent in the hearts of even pious people who are just starting out in their faith, or in their studies of spiritual matters. Snatching away a seed before it can sprout represents Satan quenching the light of faith in the heart of a person of great potential, preventing them from reaching it and thus robbing the world of a luminary who could have advanced human progress greatly, or assisted in the fight against Darkness. Lesser demons as well absolutely love to carry out these foul plans as it greatly assists Darkness directly and indirectly, as we will see in future chapters.

Again, in the parable of the weeds in Matthew 13:24–30, Jesus speaks of an enemy who sows weeds among the wheat, and in his explanation in verses 36–43, Jesus identifies the enemy as "the evil one," "the Devil" (especially Matt. 13:38–39). This is another allegory and has two related interpretations. The evil one or devil, of course, is Satan. The wheat, however, is the human race as a collective whole. "Weeds" can mean two things. In one reading, they are criminals, corrupt politicians and religious leaders, and other human evildoers who follow Satan's will of their own volition. Sometimes they can even be good people who have been corrupted by advanced demonic schemes! Satan spreads these "weeds" mixed in with the "wheat" of general humanity, good and cooperative with each other, to poison the whole batch, and to spread spiritual disease and infection so as to choke out the powers of Light within the collective. On the other hand, the weeds can also be spiritual rather than physical. They are actual demons, ghosts, and goblins, which Satan sends unnoticed into the world, just like weeds can be very hard to notice unless you know what you're looking for or are an experienced green thumb. These spiritual weeds spread unease, hatred, and dissension among people, leeching off our spiritual energy as parasites, much like parasitic weeds in botany leach nutrients from healthy plants and cause them to wither and die.

Threats to the Body and Soul

As Christ recounted in Matthew 10:28, "Do not fear those who kill the body but cannot kill the soul. Rather fear him who can destroy both soul and body in hell." As scary and terrifying as human criminals might be–axe murderers, enemy soldiers, or even just neglectful people who can kill others out of laziness or dereliction of duty–evil spiritual entities are even more terrifying; Satan most of all.

Remember, these spiritual matters, as explained in the introduction, cannot be entirely limited by even the greatest science and technology of our time. Science and technology cannot penetrate the astral realm, nor explain what happens to us after we die, and even for the most long-lived of us, we will spend much longer dead than alive!

That is why supporting the Light and fighting the Dark is so very important. With Light, even if we die—as happens to all human beings as an inevitable part of being what we are—we can enjoy God's presence and ascend to higher realities. But if Darkness wins over our hearts, we will forever be at the mercy of Satan and his evil minions. If we spurn the example of Christ, we will be dragged into Satan's domain, and there, he will tear apart our bodies and exploit our spiritual selves for his purposes, causing us levels of pain that go far beyond the physical, perverting our very souls. This is precisely why Christ warned us to "fear him" more than any other.

Emptiness Without God Is Not Neutral: It Opens the Way to Evil

Is it true that there is a middle ground between Good and Evil, Light and Dark? At first glance, it might seem so. After all, plenty of inanimate objects are in and of themselves neither good nor evil. Is there anything inherently moral about a rock sitting out in the middle of nowhere? An object like a knife seems morally neutral: If used to cook food and thus nourish people, it's good, but if used for murder, it's obviously bad. Might the same apply to people?

In truth, no. Christ told us this in Matthew 12:43-45: "When an impure spirit comes out of a person, it goes through arid places seeking rest and does not find it. Then it says, 'I will return to the house I left.' When it arrives, it finds the house unoccupied, swept clean, and put in order. Then it goes and takes with it seven other spirits more wicked than itself, and they go in and live there. And the final condition of that person is worse than the first."

Think of a 'morally neutral' person as the unoccupied house in Christ's example. When you consider a physical house, yes, such a structure would be morally neutral, neither good nor bad. For people, however, the situation is different. Someone could conceivably be morally neutral if they took actions that were neither prosocial nor antisocial, and held no strong beliefs or convictions about morality one way or another, going through life as just an automaton of sorts. But Satan and his minions are cunning and persistent, and thus, such a person is **very** vulnerable to demonic attack. As Christ told us, if He or someone else drove a single demon out of a person, their mind and soul are now "empty," but that simply allows seven demons–a far greater number–to take refuge in the empty vessel, making things much worse than before!

This is why Christ inveighed against those who are "neither cold nor hot" (Rev. 3:15-16). Given the extent to which Darkness permeates the world around us, even a seemingly neutral empty vessel can be rapidly filled by Satan's forces. This is why we must always constantly strive to be "hot," not just lukewarm, and strive to be good and righteous, not only morally neutral. The power of the Light is the only thing that can truly protect us against Darkness. Mere neutrality will end up making us pawns in its schemes.

The Lord's prayer always reminds us of this fact: "And lead us not into temptation but deliver us from evil" (Matt. 6:13). As the Supreme Good, God watches over all of His creation, both ordinary human beings like us, heroic and divine Saviors like Christ, of course, and also holy supernatural beings like angels and benevolent (as opposed to malicious) ghosts. Again, a longer description of how Light beings are organized, how to safely learn about their larger plans and the different types there are will be discussed in a different book. But for now, just keep in mind that the Lord's prayer works both to remind yourself of His existence as well as that of His benevolent servants and that even reciting the whole thing to yourself can help fortify your soul against Dark assaults and in some cases, keep lesser demons away from evil entirely–fulfilling God's promise to defend against temptation and deliver you from the Dark!

Christ's Victory Over Satan in the Wilderness

Perhaps the most exciting moment in the already enthralling saga of Christ's time on Earth is His peerless triumph over the Devil in the wilderness. This incredible feat is recounted in precisely three of the synoptic Gospels: Matthew, Mark, and Luke. The basic story is the same: Christ fasted for 40 days and nights, which rendered Him very hungry and deprived, and then the Holy Spirit led Him into the wilderness, far away from any civilization or human companionship. There, in such a pitiable state, He met Satan all by himself! Satan repeatedly tried to tempt Him away from the Light, challenging Him to turn stones to bread to eat, try and kill Himself to prove God would save him, and finally, even mastery over all the world's countries! But all three times, Christ wholeheartedly refused, restating His faith in God, and that was enough to completely foil Satan's plans and send the leader of Darkness slinking away in utter defeat.

There were many reasons for Christ's Incarnation, such as helping people directly or providing an example that humanity could look to in the future, but one of the biggest ones was precisely to defeat the Devil directly, personally, and openly—"fair and square," so to speak. This was precisely what happened in the wilderness, and it demonstrates how Christ's teaching on Earth can also be understood as two distinct but interrelated concepts.

Specifically, it explains the difference between active obedience and passive obedience to God's will, in the form of Christ's life and death, respectively. Active obedience is when you, personally, make a conscious decision, and say it out loud, to follow someone else's will. As you can see from the accounts in the Gospels, this was exactly what Christ did with Satan in the wilderness. When Satan asked Him to betray God in a specific way—turning bread to stone, throwing Himself off a building, or even accepting power over the entire world—Christ did not accept such sinful deals, and neither did He even react with violence or anger. Instead, He simply calmly rejected each of Satan's offers as incompatible with what God wanted. He actively chose to obey God's will rather than Satan's, which brought His mentality in line with the teachings of Light and banished the Devil, although, unfortunately, not for good (that will happen later, with the Second Coming). Since this active obedience did not involve sacrificing His own life, or even the risk of it, as Satan's request to fly off a building would have done, we can conclude that Christ exhibited this strategy throughout His entire life on Earth.

Passive obedience is when you go out of your way to obey, rather than reject, someone else's commands without resistance, but only because such commands (whether the person giving them realizes it or not) are actually in keeping with a larger divine plan. This is what occurred with Christ's death: Instead of fighting or trying to escape from the Roman guards who were sent to crucify Him, Christ passively obeyed their commands and went peacefully to His own death, even though it was obviously unjust (Matt. 27:11-17). This was because Christ had predicted the events, and knew exactly what His Father in Heaven had planned for the long term. Though, obviously, the rest of us human beings are not the Sons of God like Christ, and we do not share His amazing powers, we can still follow His example. When times are tough or it seems we are struggling with undue burdens, it can be good to shoulder those burdens cheerfully, and passively obey what seems at first to be unreasonable demands, as long as they don't involve hurting other people. With this spirit, the will of God can flow through you, both energizing you and preventing Satan or his minions from infesting your mind and soul, whereas miring yourself in bitterness and self-pity can render you extremely vulnerable to a demonic assault.

Be Careful! Light Attracts Darkness!

It is, after all, very true that Satan and his Dark forces are always seeking the most important and promising targets to assault, and with every success they have, their hold on the entire world grows stronger and stronger. As previously mentioned, it can be hard to perceive Dark entities, because Darkness has embedded itself so thoroughly and pervasively throughout the skein of our regular, mundane world. Our greatest, if not only, hope until Christ returns is through a collection of highly Light-attuned individuals, who are even more virtuous and heedful of God's will than most normal people. These people are like candles of Light, pushing back the Darkness of the world as much as they can on their own. You might even be one of them! But that might make you, as well as other believers and spiritually evolved people, very tempting to Satan. After all, if the Light-attuned are like candles in the darkness, Satan only has to snuff them to plunge the whole world into shadow from which it will never emerge. And, unfortunately, Satan does a very good job of this. Thus, you must always be on your guard: You might possibly have an important role to play in God's plan, and it would be a tragedy if Satan stopped you from reaching that potential.

Given this, it's quite easy to tell why Jesus Christ attracted so much demonic attention when He came to Earth. After all, in John 8:12, He did say "I am the light of the world. Whoever follows me will never walk in darkness, but will have the light of life." If even the most virtuous individuals are like candles, Jesus was like a great spotlight, burning away the Darkness with unfathomable fervor, but also serving as a gigantic beacon for them to funnel all their forces towards. While individuals might attract the attention of one or even a few demons, Jesus was attacked, or dealt with, many thousands of them; an entire Legion (as we'll explore later). Not only that, but the very head of Darkness, Satan himself, also took a personal interest in Christ! For the most part, he leaves his evil schemes to his lesser minions, so it is very rare indeed for Satan to try and corrupt someone directly. But since Jesus was such a prominent messenger of the Light, indeed *the* most prominent, Satan had essentially no choice but to intervene himself and stake everything on snuffing out not just a candle, but the very light of the world itself. And since he failed, his plot to conquer Earth and condemn all of humanity suffered a tremendous setback. Not enough to banish him forever, as he and his forces are still a very grave threat, but enough that even when Christ is no longer physically walking around Earth (although He is always with us in spirit), with the teachings of the Light, we can resist even the worst of Satan's attempts.

Casting Out Demons: Six Miracles

Christ may have beaten Satan, but even with their leader off the field, Satan's underlings still would not give up. Thus, a sizable portion of Christ's earthly ministry involved Him banishing minor demons and curing ordinary people around Galilee of demonic afflictions, proving how loving and compassionate He was.

Here are at least six instances from the New Testament where Christ bested Satan's lieutenants:

1. In Mark 1:23-26, a man in a synagogue was possessed by a single demon, who immediately recognized Christ when He arrived. With a single stern word, Christ banished the demon and saved the man.

2. In Luke 11:14, a man was rendered blind and mute by Beelzebul, one of Satan's top lieutenants and a very powerful demon in his own right. But once again, Christ easily drove him out of the man, who was able to speak and see again! However, some people thought that Christ must have been aligned with the demons to drive them out Himself, and Christ quickly and easily corrected their misconceptions, noting that if Satan's forces were divided amongst themselves, they would have been defeated a very long time ago.

3. In Matthew 8:28, Mark 5:1-20, and Luke 8:26-39, on the shores of Gadera, Jesus confronted a truly disturbed and violent man who had been possessed by not just one, but a whole army of demons. But even outnumbered as He was, the demons were absolutely no match for Him, and he expelled them from the man's body and sent them into a herd of pigs, who threw themselves into the water of a nearby lake and drowned. The demons referred to themselves as "Legion," which today is a word referring to an army of soldiers, but back in Roman times meant at least ten thousand specifically. This shows how truly powerful Christ was!

4. In Matthew 9:32, Jesus quickly exercised another mute man and was also accused of dealing with the Devil, a charge He refuted as easily as he did the one mentioned in Luke.

5. In Matt. 15:21-28 and Mark 7:24-30, a Gentile, or non-Jewish woman (specifically of the Syrophoenician ethnic group) begged Jesus to save her daughter from a possession. Jesus initially refused, saying He was only brought to Israel, but when the woman revealed her deep

faith, Jesus promptly banished the demon away. This shows how Christ came to save all of humanity, not just a single ethnic group, even if the Jewish Old Testament in particular was the blessed product of the gifted and tenacious Jewish people. It also shows that demons do not discriminate on skin color or place of birth–no matter who you are, you are at risk, which makes following Christ's example and letting Light energies into your heart so important!

6. In the final instance of Him healing a child, Matt. 17:14-18, Mark 9:14-29, and Luke 9:38-42 describe Jesus hearing a request from the desperate father of a young boy living near the foot of Mount Hermon. The boy was afflicted by a demon who would cause him to throw himself into fire, water, and other dangerous situations. Christ offered to save the lad if the father believed, and the father asked him to "help [his] unbelief." Without further ado, Christ banished the demon and the boy was saved. This illustrates two things: First, the demons are not just spiritually dangerous, but physically as well. They can control your body and cause you to do physical harm to your own flesh and blood, and in extreme situations, they can even make you end your own life! Yet another reason to be so careful of them. Secondly, even though it can be hard to believe in the supernatural, benevolent beings like Christ can help you through it, and by seeking their protection and avoiding demons, even if you don't have much experience with spiritual matters, you can at least protect yourself from those who wish to harm you.

The Unseen Realms of Demons, Evil Spirits, and Ghosts

I f you consider the Bible to be generally historically accurate, it is indisputable that demons exist. Even beyond the Bible, from a moral point of view, it is equally indisputable that good and evil exist, and that there are actions human beings should and should not take. The Devil and his demons, according to the Biblical account, encourage us towards the latter, and thus in that same account was one of Christ's primary purposes to come to Earth to fight them and save us from them. But even the most fervent believer might have a few questions: Why did God not destroy Lucifer, Satan and all evil angels? Is there a purpose behind allowing evil to exist? We will discuss this in the last chapter.

After all, He is omniscient, and He surely would have been able to predict that Satan would go astray, lead others astray, and eventually fall entirely. Such a seemingly pointless tragedy is very hard for ordinary humans to understand, but you must remember that this is due entirely to our limited knowledge and perspective. It is possible there is some unknown good God is drawing out of Satan's rebellion, one which could not exist if he had not rebelled, and one that even he is unaware of himself. The only thing we can know for certain is that all happens in accordance with God's will.

The Forces of Darkness

Many demons, as described earlier, were originally angels serving in God's heavenly host–He created them and approximately a third of those fell to Darkness behind Satan.

Trapped on Earth due to their disobedience, the very nature of their beings had changed: Due to their own decisions, and due to their focus on pride and spite rather than Light-oriented emotions like altruism and service to God, these former angels became twisted and ugly both spiritually and, as we might perceive them, physically. They are tortured and hateful, blaming God for their woes, and thus seek to spitefully foil His plans however they can. Even if they are doomed to fail, and some know they are, they are so miserable that just delaying God's plans is enough for them. Anything to hurt Him.

This is why these demons are so inimical to humanity. As sentient beings, we play a very special role in God's plans for all of creation. As beautiful as the universe He created might have been, it would still be cold and empty if no beings were around to enjoy it. Thus, God created us through the process of gradual evolution, producing sapient, conscious beings over the course of millions of years who were capable of learning about God's grand design and bringing Him joy through appreciating it. And as conscious beings, rather than mindless tools unable to freely choose to love Him, we could also be His true friends and companions.

For mere humble creatures like us to bring God such happiness fills Satan and his jealous legions with rage. They cannot tolerate our closeness to the Light from which they have been banished! Thus do the demons harry us physically, mentally, and spiritually. It's bad enough they afflict us with diseases, as was the case with the many Biblical examples of deafness, muteness, etc. we discussed earlier, but they also try to implant their own rage, spite, selfishness, and hatred into our hearts, in ways subtle and direct. They may try to drive us insane, or simply turn us angry and bitter, and thus closed off to higher spiritual realities and the forces of Light. Not only would this make Christ's army weaker both in terms of numbers and forces generated during the Second Coming (as we will discuss later), but it also gives the demons pleasure–such as they have–to watch unfortunate humans in pain.

But as with all things, even this evil serves a role in God's providence. The harrying of humanity by Lucifer's demonic forces serves as a sort of "experiment" for God. The details of it are, again, far beyond the scope of this book, though reading on the subject of theodicy (the problem of evil) can provide some answers. The important thing to remember is that even as He came to earth to keep things from getting out of hand, Christ permitted this "experiment" to continue, which is why we still have demonic possessions and attacks today. Christ's reasons for doing so, much like God's, are beyond human comprehension; all we know is two things: First is that He must have a very good reason for permitting it. Second, and equally important, we know that this experiment has a pre-ordained and divinely dictated end date–it will not last forever.

However long it takes, and however dark things seem to get (both metaphorically and literally!) we know beyond any doubt that Christ will eventually return and put a stop to Satan's schemes once and for all. That will end the experiment, also liberating humanity, and whatever evil was caused by Satan will be outweighed a hundredfold by the glory God will somehow successfully obtain.

Where Do Dark Entities Live?

Even though they were expelled from Heaven, Satan, and his demons do not live on Earth *entirely* physically. If Hell were actually a physical place, one you could just drive or fly to, it would be very easy to escape it and even destroy it! No, the true location from which demons come is much more abstract.

Demons reside on what is called the astral plane. It is sort of a middle ground between our mundane, physical world and the lowest level of the heavens, where some of God's angels reside. If the physical is the lowest level, the astral is the second lowest and overlaps with the physical in many places.

By the same token, the bodies of demons themselves are sort of in-between purely material and non-material. Humans are physical creatures, but we can with training perceive spiritual beings. Demons instantiate the properties of both at the same time. They can appear at specific physical locations and take forms intelligible to people, in some cases even able to manipulate physical objects or make sounds like creatures would. However, much of their being also resides on the astral plane, so even if one were to see a demon, *and* recognize it as such, you wouldn't be able to destroy it with guns or swords or other physical means. These types of things called "semi-material," have to be firmly dealt with only on the non-material level. Christ was able to do this thanks to His supreme spiritual powers, but for the rest of us, it is very important not to confront demons directly, even when you think you can see them, without the aid of a trained exorcist or holy person.

Another way to think of it that might be easier to understand is through the concept of dimensions. We are all familiar with length, height, and width as the dimensions of physical space. However, consider the spiritual realm as a higher dimension. The astral realm would be like a dimension above the 3rd dimension. And since that is where demons live, they seem to have powers unimaginable to us, sort of like how a person living in a two-dimensional realm, like a piece of paper, would find someone in a three-dimensional realm—one with height as well as length and width—to have unimaginable power.

Darkness Hierarchy

Finally, demons do have a hierarchy of their own, a Dark mockery of God's angelic hierarchy. Since they are very secretive, and it is very dangerous to study them, no one is entirely certain how great the hierarchy is or how many levels it specifically has. We do know of a general outline, however. At the top, of course, is Satan himself, the leader of all the demons. He is the King of Hell. Below him are the great Princes, who serve as his council and advisors, and who themselves command legions of lesser demons. Beelzebul, whose Bible story we recounted earlier, is one such Prince, whose entire Legion—many thousands strong—was driven away by Christ. Below the princes are Barons, who are both powerful and intelligent, and thus carry out the specifics of the broad, general plan the Princes give them. Demonic Knights are the leaders of small detachments of demons, not very strong and only trusted by the Barons with the most simple, specific tasks. And below those are individual demons, too weak and considered too unworthy for anything other than following the straight, direct orders of the Knights. These pitiful creatures are used for the most menial tasks like harassing individual people or, in some cases, causing poltergeist-like phenomena. While individually their tricks do not mean much, collectively, many of them working under the Knights, who themselves are working under the command of Barons, can cause a great deal of trouble and lead to many unwary souls being taken by the Dark.

As a last note, I hasten to add that these titles are gender-neutral, as demons are both male and female. Some were male or female angels before they fell from God's grace, but many others are entirely Satan's creation–since his forces only account for a third of God, through very evil methods, Satan learned how to create his own demons out of nothing but spiritual energy rather than perverting beings God had already made. These "new" demons are male and female as well. Dark forces pay no heed to gender, so men and women both should always be on their guard and never allow Satan or his minions to gain even a foothold into their hearts!

More About Demons, Evil Spirits, and Ghosts

Now that we have established the existence of Satan, his rebellion against Christ and God, and the many legions of creatures who have joined him in that rebellion, we can get into more specific details about how many different types of such creatures he employs, the differences between those types, and how to detect each one. There are three large categories of supernatural entities that encompass more than ninety percent of those that people usually encounter in their day-to-day lives. They are demons, evil spirits, and ghosts. The remaining ten percent cannot be easily classified into those categories, but can still be understood in terms more or less familiar to a contemporary person well-versed in folklore, or even pop culture: Such creatures are often called ghouls, ghasts, goblins, or gremlins.

Demons

Demons have played the largest part in the story we have told thus far. These creatures are fallen angels (most of them have long pre-existed mankind) who consciously chose the path of darkness. As mentioned above, Satan was able to turn about one-third of the angels God created against Him, and along with Satan, these form almost all of the most powerful demons which attempt to corrupt humanity.

Now, it is true that some demons, and even a minority of powerful ones, were created afterward. Some of these have even undergone human birth. In some cases, through extremely dark arts, the most depraved and corrupt human villains were able to "ascend," or, more accurately, descend into demonhood, shedding both their mortal bodies as well as their kindness, compassion, and very humanity itself in return for false promises of power Satan whispered in their ears. In other cases, demons trying to ruin the natural course of human events projected their minds and their black souls from the astral plane to the physical one, enmeshing themselves into the bodies of otherwise entirely innocent fetuses or, occasionally, newborns, and taking them over, blending in with humanity blissfully unaware of their existence and plans.

These demons are very intelligent and are easily capable of destroying entire nations. It is not for no reason that Beelzebul, for instance, was able to command an entire legion of lesser demons. Their intellect, combined with their immense age (in most cases) and knowledge of the deepest secrets of both Light and Dark, has allowed them to carry out some of the worst tragedies recounted in not only the Bible, but human history: Many great wars, massacres, and other instances of mass death have had more than a bit of demonic influence, with powerful and cunning demons manipulating economies, societies, and politics to subtly push entire countries away from Divine teachings of love and charity, resulting in great states going to war with each other rather than finding peaceful solutions to problems. Naturally, demons tend to look for individual humans or entire countries and cultures which have the most influence on the rest of the world, and try to subvert those first. The strongest demons are also the most power-hungry and often demand sacrifices (such as small children or babies!) which we will describe later.

One of the primary reasons powerful demons are able to do this is because of their incredible shape-changing abilities. Most of us are familiar with animals that can disguise themselves, such as octopi or chameleons, which can change their colors to blend in with the environment. If they possess a human being, demons can give their host the same ability through their astral powers. Again, they need to possess someone to do this—that is to say, they need some kind of physical substrate to work with. However, once they have that, demons can give themselves virtually any form or aspect we can imagine! The host's gender or appearance does not matter: He or she can take the guise of a man or a woman, big or small, hideously ugly or (more often) heart-stoppingly beautiful, of any race or ethnicity is known throughout all of history. They can also sound like anyone of any gender, and copy any necessary ways of moving, gesturing, or any other physical mannerism as well. This is conjecture on my part to an extent–I have not personally witnessed these sorts of transformations. However, I am aware of Dark rituals or techniques which should allow demons to carry them out.

Frighteningly, this makes it very easy for demons to appear as false prophets. People have a tendency to believe the best of those who look handsome or beautiful, and an even more pronounced tendency to fall under the sway of those who have beautiful voices. It's easy to believe that physical beauty proves a person has God's favor. Demons are able to exploit this aspect of human psychology by disguising themselves as the prettiest human beings possible, and then pretending to speak for God, while in truth preaching lies that outrightly subvert His will! It is incredibly cunning as well as immoral and mendacious, but it does illustrate the lengths to which demons are willing to go in their fight against God. As you can imagine, many horrible crusades and religious conflicts have been started by demonic false prophets, who sow dissension and hatred among religions rather than peace and love between all of them, creating devastating wars where the various faiths should have instead been working together to better understand God in their various ways. Some of these false prophets have even worked to hinder translations, preservations, or distributions of the Bible, audaciously using the name of God to stop His word from being spread!

It can be very difficult for human beings to distinguish between good and evil leaders, whether they are religious or secular. It would be hard even if demons were not constantly trying to deceive and mislead us! This is why we must always sharpen our critical thinking skills, and never believe what a famous person or celebrity says just because they happen to be well-known, influential, or physically beautiful. Always use your own moral judgment and knowledge of the Bible, and if someone says something that contradicts what you know to be right or what you know the Bible says, they may be trying to lead you into Darkness, whether they are a demon or not.

A very high number of people have been taken to the grave by false prophets, both of the demonic kind and ordinary human deceivers. Demons, however, are immensely terrifying for another reason: Unlike ordinary humans, even the worst of whom are only capable of destroying one's body, demons are capable of capturing and destroying your *soul* as well. And just as Christ said in the quote from Matthew 10:28 you undoubtedly recall, that is a far worse fate than just the destruction of the body. The soul is that through which you can connect to higher spiritual realities and eventually God himself. The physical body is really the lowest and least important part of a human being, and though you should take care of it, the health of the soul is always the most important thing. Thus, a demon that can destroy your soul can punish you in a way far worse than even the most painful bodily torture. Yet another reason to watch out for demons as much as possible!

Evil Spirits

These are somewhat of a strange case. They are definitely related to demons and fallen angels and have more knowledge of spiritual matters and the existence of God than many humans. However, they are not exactly as powerful as demons tend to be–they do not have the same powers of shape-shifting, nor do they have as much ancient knowledge as truly fallen angels have. You might be able to consider these sort of a halfway point between humans and demons, due to them definitely being related to the latter in some ways, but possessing some of the weaknesses of the former.

Evil spirits typically manifest as what seems at first glance to be naked apparitions, especially around tombs or other places of death. When Jesus resurrected, there were many of these beings surrounding His empty tomb, which He had to banish to keep His disciples as well as the women who initially saw Him as safe as possible.

At a distance, evil spirits can be mistaken for naked human beings, or occasionally ghosts (to be discussed in the next section), because they seem to have a more or less human shape: They typically seem as if they have a head, a torso, two arms, and two legs. Only that general shape is visible; they usually don't seem to be wearing any clothes, and their color is usually a pale white, occasionally grey. However, when you get closer, even an ordinary person can tell they're not human at all. Their "faces" are featureless and the proportions of their bodies are all wrong, with the arms and legs either far too short or too long for actual humans. They are surrounded by a dim glow, but an ominous one rather than a reassuring one, as the auras of angels (and very Light-aligned people) possess.

While these creatures thankfully cannot corrupt or destroy souls like demons can, they are still very dangerous and diabolical. Specifically, they are capable of draining human life force and killing people that way. You may be familiar with vampires or other bloodsucking creatures from folklore and pop culture. Evil spirits are similar in that they drain our spiritual energy in order to sustain themselves–in other words, they are parasites incapable of living on their own unless they feed off of us.

Evil spirits–and demons as well, as we will see in the next chapter–require specific conditions to do the most damage. First, they need physical bodies to carry out physical actions, and both creatures often travel around looking for the perfect hosts they can possess and infest. Those hosts most often have holes in their subtle energy systems. If you are not strong in faith or if you don't trust in Heaven or God, that provides an opening for both demons and evil spirits to bypass your psychological and spiritual defenses and suck you dry. Also, if you are emotionally disturbed–very depressed, very angry, consumed by negative emotions, and so on–that's practically an open invitation for Darkness to take you over! Finally, uneducated and weak minds are easy targets. Generally, we see mostly uneducated people being possessed much more than doctors/engineers/entrepreneurs. Investing in education and good schools can be a surprisingly effective way to fend off many Dark incursions.

The above-described factors are passive weaknesses that increase your risks of being attacked by Dark forces. There are also things you actively choose to do that can massively increase those risks, however: Practicing occult techniques and trying to communicate with "the other side" without proper supervision. Things like Ouija boards might seem like fun diversions, but they can be immensely dangerous if you don't know what you're doing. You will make yourself a "beacon" to spiritual forces, and most of them will mean you ill! Thus, should you ever wish to experiment with contacting ghosts or spirits, I strongly recommend you only do so with the assistance of an experienced priest or missionary or an exorcist.

Evil spirits create sort of an astral vacuum near their locations in the physical world, draining the life energy of people and animals there. Since this life energy is also required for physical health, creatures drained of it seem to wither and die without any physical explanation—a coroner will not be able to find any wounds, poisons, or diseases that could explain it. This is why evil spirits like lurking near tombs, graveyards, and other places of death. If you see many non-human corpses, such as dead birds or especially dead deer or larger animals, in a graveyard where people are as well, you should be extremely careful of an evil spirit nearby and leave as soon as you possibly can.

Gremlins

These are small evil creatures, far weaker than demons, and even weaker than ghosts and evil spirits, that can attach themselves to a person or to organic things and cause harm. In most cases, Gremlins are controlled directly by more powerful entities. Their Dark masters usually send them on some small tasks like causing unexplained glitches (losing keys or documents, computer crashes, car accidents, leaks in pipes, and other kinds of minor but expensive plumbing issues, and so on).

Much worse, however, is how gremlins can incite humans to violence without directly controlling them. They are sometimes responsible for shootings in schools or religious gatherings, or other kinds of violent gun usage. The evil entities whisper constantly into the ears of the person to commit an act like "Take the gun and kill people in the school." Unfortunately, we have seen an increase in these sorts of incidents recently. We are living in desperate times, and the Darkness is equally desperate as Light for an upper hand in the contest for Earth's souls.

Ghosts

Ghosts are, as everyone is familiar with these days, the spirits of human beings who have died but have not entirely left the physical world. However, there are two differences between them and demons you may not be aware of. First, ghosts are not necessarily or inherently evil. Again, you may be familiar with such good entities from media like *Casper the Friendly Ghost*, where the little spirit was kind and helpful rather than malevolent. Obviously, in real life, "friendly ghosts" don't look anything like Casper, but they do exist and try to guide and assist humans rather than hurt them. However, since this book is about the Dark and how to protect yourself from it, we won't discuss good ghosts here; that is something for future work. For now, the other salient difference between ghosts and demons is that the former are exclusively human beings who have died. The vast majority of demons are fallen angels or created by Satan, and while a handful are humans who have transformed themselves, ghosts are—every last one of them—normal humans who underwent no transformation or sublimation. They are simply people who died as humans do (sometimes naturally, sometimes violently), who are still strongly attached to the places of their deaths, or who have unfinished business on Earth. In other words, they possess humanity that demons lack, whether they never had it in the first place (having been created directly by God, but abandoned Him) or left it behind (transforming into demons through Dark arts).

What sort of unfinished business keeps the spirit or astral body of a human being connected to the physical realm? Depending on its nature, it also affects the temperament of the ghost. If someone died while desperately wanting to pass a message to a loved one, it can result in them staying as a mournful apparition who wants attention, but not necessarily a violent one. On the other hand, if someone died a violent death, a strong desire for revenge being their "unfinished business" can make them violent themselves.

In general, if someone dies while still having something that very strongly attaches them to life, that they absolutely didn't want to lose–whether it's a loved one, or extreme hatred and resentment for an injustice done to them–that will keep them here even after death. People who die peacefully, or after accomplishing everything they wanted, with no deep attachments (either positive or negative) to this world can usually pass on much more easily.

This leads to the most significant and notorious kind of ghostly encounter: "Intelligent hauntings." This is when a person who's died maintained at least a part of their intelligence and personality even when trapped between this physical realm and the afterlife, consciously interacting with the world as a disembodied spirit in order to achieve some specific goal. These beings make their presence known in more ways than one, and they are very often upset with you, specifically, should they encounter you (friendly ghosts might want to help you). Time is irrelevant to such beings: They can wait for decades, or occasionally even centuries, in order to give you a scare (or worse!) if that's what it takes to achieve their goal. Whether it's your family, the family after yours, or a great great great great grandchild, they are in it for the long haul.

You should be very careful around such beings, and avoid certain locations if they seem to be bound to a specific place, or consult a priest or exorcist if they seem to follow you around. Very vengeful ghosts, while not consciously serving the Dark, can still cause you physical pain and attempt to injure you by throwing objects at you (poltergeist activity) if you draw their ire. Sometimes, if it is possible, research can reveal why they are haunting you or the area, and it can be a very virtuous deed to solve whatever problem is binding a ghost to the world: For instance, helping to catch a murderer whose vengeful victim cannot rest in peace. But again, this is something best left to the most skilled and trained personnel.

Before we move on to Eastern demons, however, we should discuss one more type of ghostly activity known as "residual haunting." These are usually completely harmless, and totally unrelated to the struggle between Christ and the Light and demons and the Dark, but just so you're not confused by such occurrences we should briefly describe them here.

These are essentially "blasts from the past." When an event produces an extreme amount of psychic energy–usually from a large mass of people, so typically the sites of large battles or, in unhappier cases, mass murder–sometimes the huge amount of collective astral energy released is enough to leave a lasting imprint on the physical world as well, even after the bodies of all involved have decayed. In this case, the imprint is very much like a film or movie, but one that has somehow been absorbed into a house or some other kind of environment rather than a screen. The end result is the same, though: It's been preserved for your viewing pleasure, so don't be afraid or panicked, just sit back, grab your popcorn, and enjoy. The most notorious examples of these residuals are the continued sightings of Union and Confederate soldiers in the United States, in historical battlefields of the American Civil War.

Demons in the Eastern Tradition

So far we have discussed conceptions of ghosts and demons that are most familiar to Westerners: Americans or Europeans at least living in a distinctively European-flavored Christian context. However, demonic activity has also been long known to people in Asia and Africa, and these cultures' perspectives on it can also provide many helpful tips to keep you safe, as well as dire warnings about what can happen if one does not identify the agents of Darkness as quickly and accurately as possible.

For whatever reason, demons seem to be much more common in the East these days. Stories about possessions, demonic manifestations, and so on are almost a weekly if not daily sight in that region, causing a lot of drama in many of the more active churches I have seen, while almost vanishingly rare in Europe and America. It would be too much of a digression into sociology and maybe history for me to go into the reasons that this might be the case. However, I can tell you quite a bit about what I have seen personally.

In the West, we don't typically see exorcisms performed in real life very often. In fact, for the vast majority of people, their only knowledge of the subject comes from the famous horror movie, *The Exorcist*, or other more modern ones. In the East, however, I have personally witnessed exorcisms in rural and village churches almost every week. It can often get very physical and abusive–ironically enough, this is one aspect of the ritual that Western movies have depicted with pinpoint accuracy. The exorcisms usually invoke the Name of Christ, but they still get very nasty, often involving the beating of the afflicted with brooms and slippers.

There are hundreds of stories I could tell you about this, some with happier endings than others. But to keep things brief, I will only say that "there is an antidote to every 'dote." In all cases, the villagers tried to use methods of the Light most inimical to demonic forces–the antidote–but sometimes the "dote" of darkness was just too strong. Sometimes the evil spirits just would not relinquish their grasp on the afflicted person no matter the exorcist's efforts. In that case, as another saying goes, sometimes to remove a thorn, you have to use another thorn. I have seen a few desperate exorcists try very unconventional methods to banish powerful demons, like abusing and pulling the hair of possessed persons–but I will spare you those details, as even in a book about demons, they may be too disturbing for the common reader.

An equally disturbing fact, but one that I cannot leave out, is that in some very isolated village churches, they actually *worship* demons. As mentioned above, demons are very good at shape-shifting and appear as incredibly charismatic humans. Sometimes they can even fake supernatural activity that makes it seem like they are still aligned with the Light. In either case, they can trick many uneducated or unaware people into worshiping them rather than God. It is an extremely tragic and dangerous situation. Such cases can be very difficult nuts to crack for individuals, and if you suspect a church or congregation has been subverted by or is worshiping a demon, you should work with a larger, organized denomination in the area to perform a professional exorcism, if necessary, or hopefully loosen the hold of the demon through gentler means and gradually bring the misled innocents back into Biblical orthodoxy.

False Teachers and False Prophets

This is a subject I have personal experience with as well. One of my first teachers, who taught me some important concepts about God, Christ, Heaven, and meditation, seemed like a true holy man, with a peaceful and soothing smile, radiant with the power and wisdom of the Light. My studies with this person seemed to go well for a few years until a psychic person pointed out that there were dark hooks in my astral energy system. I was able to see them psychically as well. I removed them, but this former teacher kept putting them back. I had to fight to remove these controlling claws from my system. There are higher-level beings that seem to serve the Light on an external level that is actually controlling you and will take you down at an appropriate time. These are high-level Dark beings.

Recall there are many prophets who had committed mass suicide. There are many prophets in the world today that hook you with their teachings and their energies, and you may not be able to recognize the filters in your mind. This is a cause of great sadness among the Heavenly hosts.

Weapons of Darkness

The Bible warns of Satan's grave threat to humanity by referring to him as "the god of this age" (2 Corinthians 4:4) who "prowls" the earth "looking for someone to devour" (1 Peter 5:8). Demons are no less dangerous, as the Bible describes them as: "impure spirits" (Mark 1:27), "deceiving spirit(s)" (1 Kings 22:23), "the powers of this dark world" and "the spiritual forces of evil" (Ephesians 6:12), and as Satan's "angels" (Revelation 12:9). Calling them dangerous is one thing, but in what ways specifically can they threaten our health and well-being? This chapter will describe the various schemes, diabolical instruments, and devilish techniques the forces of Darkness use to assail us, and how you can use specific weapons of Light to shield yourself from each one.

Biblical Advice

In the Bible, demons harm humans primarily through the method of possession, which we have discussed briefly in an earlier chapter, "Threats to Body and Soul." As you will recall from our various examples, demonic possession can make people blind, mute, or deaf; give them convulsions and make them foam at the mouth or gnash their teeth; give them extraordinary, superhuman strength which they can use to hurt others; a very fierce, combative demeanor; and cause them to exhibit self-destructive behavior like trying to drown or burn themselves. Many experienced missionaries in Africa, South America, and Asia have described how demon-possessed people can seem like entirely different individuals, with no trace of their original personalities. It is truly terrifying!

The worst of all, however, is when demons control people in such a way that it's not immediately obvious they are being possessed–they don't seem to be immediately harmed, nor do they start acting extremely strangely–but rather cause them to carry out demonic plans that further the very long-term designs of Darkness. The greatest example of this evil scheme was in Luke 22:3-6: "Then Satan entered Judas, called Iscariot, one of the Twelve. And Judas went to the chief priests and the officers of the temple guard and discussed with them how he might betray Jesus. They were delighted and agreed to give him money."

The very leader of Darkness himself personally possessed one of Jesus' own apostles and coerced him into betraying his Lord. The evil of the act was so profound that Judas' soul was perpetually condemned! It could have spelled the end of Light on Earth, but thankfully, for all his cunning, Satan could not have comprehended Christ's plans and did not realize that Jesus anticipated His own death and knew He would end up resurrected, turning what would have been an epic Dark victory into a triumph for Light. Still, such serendipity is not at all common. Most of the time, when demons commandeer someone, the plans they carry out can lead to many Light-aligned souls being snuffed out, and much despair and destruction spreading across the world overall.

How to Detect if a Person is Possessed

There are ways to detect if someone has been possessed in addition to the violent and self-harming activities described above:

- Radical personality changes almost overnight (from being good to not too good).

- Insatiable hunger: The person craves food; eats a lot of food, but the food does not really nourish or appear in their physical body. This food is consumed by the evil spirit within.

- New and terrifying sexual appetites. Some evil entities love sex because of the emotions attached to it. There are many dark underground places where these predators thrive.

- The person becomes abusive suddenly and then behaves well at other times.

- The person becomes much more impulsive and seems to lose all sense of self-control, like having a split personality.

- The person starts talking in a different voice, usually deeper and more guttural or unpleasant, but sometimes higher-pitched and almost alluring.

- The person displays supernatural knowledge of subjects (material, spiritual, or historical) they should know nothing about.

- The person may suddenly appear with a slew of new abilities they could not possibly have learned in a short time, like becoming an expert public speaker, driver, or other professional skills.

Personal Experiences in My Family

I have known the pain of this sort of possession very keenly in my own life: Both my father and grandmother have had incidents with Evil spirits.

Case of My Grandmother

My grandmother had been bedridden for more than five years and passed away a year ago as of the time of this book's publication. During the last two years of her life, she was verbally very abusive to everyone who came to visit her. This was because she had been possessed by an evil spirit that visited her at random times. This particular evil spirit possessed her tongue, making her very verbally abusive. After a few hours, when the evil spirit left her, she went back to being the nicest person you could ever meet and did not recollect any bad things she had said.

My mother, who is very pious (she is an extremely faith-based person who trusts Christ for everything), is definitely the most Christ-centric person I have ever known. She has a gift of prayer and healing. People in the neighborhood come to take her blessings for auspicious occasions such as Marriage, Birthdays, Student exam days, Healings...etc. Even her prayers were not able to get this evil spirit out of her own mother. Both my mother and I prayed and many local pastors and religious leaders too, but to no avail: No matter what we did, this did not stop the evil spirit from possessing my grandmother's tongue.

I considered myself a failure in this scenario, but looking back on it now, it seems to be proof that there are some things God allows to happen, that are beyond our human comprehension. Perhaps this was the case with my grandmother.

Case of My Father

My father passed away when I was three years old. I was born in a very small town back in the Eastern Hemisphere. My Father was possessed either by a demon or an evil spirit. I was too young to remember all of this, so most of the incidents were related to me by my father's siblings (my paternal aunts and uncles) and my mother. My father also left a diary detailing all his unusual encounters. It is clear that he had the gift of psychic ability as he could see these spiritual entities and also interact with them in some way. His diary indicated many instances of demons or spirits following him when he used to walk alone at night after work. Seems unbelievable in these modern days.

For reasons of family privacy, I cannot go into much detail here, but I can mention a couple of things. He always used to tell my mother that he could see a girl outside in the backyard on the swing, and the swing was moving, but no one else could see her. Also sometimes when my parents came into our house they saw the food dishes all messed up and all the furniture in disarray, even though no one could have entered. On the day he died, my father possessed incredible strength, so that six men had to pin him down while the priest was performing an exorcism. When the priest failed, local shamans were involved with their techniques as well. Alas, the evil proved too strong and unfortunately this ended in his death.

Weapons of Darkness

For all the various ways they harry us, Satan and his demons have a single overriding goal: To destroy us, separate us from God, and keep us from enjoying His presence in Heaven. Other subtle, stealthy ways demons do this include:

Targeting Believers

Concentrating on unbelievers rather than believers. In many cases, demons will pollute the minds of atheists and agnostics rather than trying to mislead Christians or other followers of Abrahamic faiths directly. As 2 Corinthians 4:4 says, "The god of this age has blinded the minds of unbelievers, so that they cannot see the light of the gospel that displays the glory of Christ, who is the image of God." What this means is that Satan and his minions are making unbelievers or people you may want to convert unreasonably skeptical. Not so much so that their personalities seem radically different, but just subtly clouding their minds so that no evidence—scriptural or otherwise—you can provide, for the truth of their faith will convince them.

By maintaining their unbelief, demons make them more vulnerable to the darkness later on even if they don't directly assault such people immediately, and even worse, such stubborn skepticism can sometimes weaken the faith of less experienced missionaries.

Deceit

Another demonic weapon is deceit, as described in the previous chapter. As it is said in 2 Corinthians 11:14-15, "Satan himself masquerades as an angel of light. It is not surprising, then, if his servants also masquerade as servants of righteousness. Their end will be what their actions deserve." Demons, using their shape-changing abilities to pose as holy men or accomplished missionaries, can cause great damage by spreading lies about the faith while making people think they are faithful. This was also foretold in the Bible in 1 Timothy 4:1 and Revelation 16:14: "The Spirit clearly says that in later times some will abandon the faith and follow deceiving spirits and things taught by demons" and "They are demonic spirits that perform signs, and they go out to the kings of the whole world, to gather them for the battle on the great day of God Almighty."

Idolatry

One of the keys to detecting such perfidy is the presence of idolatry. No matter how wise, just, or compassionate a religious leader or preacher seems to be, if they start telling you to give sacrifices to statues or worship inanimate objects, they are *definitely* trying to lead you down the wrong path and might well be either a demon in disguise or possessed by one. Scripture tells us that demons are very strongly associated with these kinds of practices: In fact, in at least five passages (there are many more), the Bible describes misguided Israelites even sacrificing their own children to demons! See Leviticus 17:7, Deuteronomy 32:17, 2 Chronicles 11:15, Psalm 106:37, and Zechariah 13:2.

Causing Trouble and Pain

Finally, demons will sometimes just attach themselves to a person and cause incessant, incurable supernatural pain. They often do this to the strongest believers, in order to test how strong someone's faith truly is. As also written in 2 Corinthians 2:17, "Therefore, in order to keep me from becoming conceited, I was given a thorn in my flesh, a messenger of Satan, to torment me." Now, the demons themselves do this in order to break people's faith, in the hopes they will abandon God. However, the author of 2 Corinthians, Paul, was an enormously pious man, and he states that the demon tormented him so that he would not grow conceited.

This shows how wise God is and how everything is part of His plan: In many cases, demons causing you pain are allowed to do so by God, because He knows you will overcome the hardship and strengthen your faith once the demon is banished. Thus, always trust in God and remember that He is the author of the universe and its story, with even your misfortunes being part of that story that will lead to greater glory.

Other Demonic Weapons

The Bible certainly contains much wisdom, but even that great book did not describe every single weapon in Satan's arsenal. Here we will describe some other lesser-known calamities Darkness occasionally wreaks upon the world.

Targets Emotional Disturbed Persons

First, Darkness thrives in emotional wrecks and in emotionally disturbed environments. Ranging from poorly run hospitals and insane asylums, these places can serve as breeding grounds for demons and dark spirits. They may not necessarily be sentient or have wills of their own, but if so, much negativity coalesces around them, and the people inside will inevitably be affected, rendering them easy prey for devils–and this a very attractive target. Avoid such places when you can, and if possible, enlist the aid of professionals, and if necessary even exorcists, to reduce the dysfunction that allows emotional distress to run rampant in an area. This will strike a blow for Light against the Dark!

Use of Technology

Darkness also evolves with time and experience. Demons are also not Luddites–they will happily use modern technology to spread deceit and lies. You have almost certainly heard of programs like ChatGPT, or AIs that can mimic people's voices. While these impressive technologies might have legitimate uses, demons are also utilizing them, either directly or by possessing or influencing programmers and computer scientists, to falsify Scripture, make fake recordings of what seem to be holy people, or just spread all kinds of misinformation in order to sow chaos and discord in the world. Always use your critical thinking whenever you see anything online, and always make sure there's a way to verify any audio or video you receive, to avoid falling prey to not only human scammers but demonic ones as well!

Physical Damage

You should also be careful of just basic, simple physical attacks. Though demons rarely do this, when they are very desperate, they can channel their astral energies into the physical world to throw objects around like poltergeists do, or even manifest claws and teeth to attack pious agents of the Light. Although only the most powerful demons can actually kill a human being in this way, always gird yourself with prayers and Light energies. Demons can hurt you physically, but you won't be able to respond in the same way, since so much of their existence is on higher spiritual planes. By fighting them on that level you can protect yourself on the physical level as well.

Drain Your Energies

Finally, demons can torment your soul in a similar fashion to how evil spirits lurking around tombs can operate, but demons are stronger and thus their energy-leaching is even more dangerous. Even worse, they themselves grow stronger by draining yours! What happens is that demons search for people who are not entirely dedicated to the Light and have allowed Darkness into their hearts, even in a small way. Your energy signature in the astral world reflects the health of your soul and its balance between Light and Dark, and demons have exceptional astral sight that allows them to find weaknesses in that signature. They hone in towards those cracks and holes in your spiritual reflection, latch on to these 'spiritual holes' and start draining your life energy. When this happens, they can often grow in size and power by obtaining that Dark-aligned energy, which is how some weak demons (not a huge amount, thankfully, but some), which were created long after Satan's initial rebellion, gradually grew to become as powerful as some of his lieutenants who were originally created by God!

How Dark Forces Influence the World

Representatives of darkness will invariably follow Satan's teachings in the end, as described in chapter one; egoism (service to self), boxing people in, growing at the cost of others, turning people into mere sheep to be exploited, and so on. This section highlights some of these tactics used by dark forces. I am purposefully keeping this short to not cross the fine line of truth vs conspiracy theories.

The descriptions are general guidelines, not absolute rules— there have been scientists, teachers, and gurus who spread teachings of darkness, and politicians and monarchs who have spread the Light. A more reliable guide for telling them apart revolves around the specific actions such leaders may take and the goals they work towards. Also, keep in mind that it can be very difficult to tell if an individual is an agent of either side in disguise or simply in contact with such a spiritual agent, or indirectly controlled by one.

Boxing people and removing freedom

Servants of the Dark will try to pass laws or enact social policies that reduce individual freedom and make it harder for people to break free of a system. While total freedom might lead to anarchy, Dark ones try to reduce freedom in ways that do not lead to greater safety or prosperity for society. Restrictions on free speech, religion, or travel, laws upholding racial discrimination, and so on, are the sorts of things Dark leaders favor

Growing at the cost of others

Dark societies are usually organized around the lines of social Darwinism. Rather than the individuals who make up a community helping each other with their problems, Dark leaders will encourage them to make money or cultivate influence by keeping others down and stabbing each other in the back, ostensibly so only the 'strongest' will rise to the top while the 'weaker' perish. This is the essence of Satan's egoistic "Service to Self" ideals; only working for oneself without regard for anyone else, even if you have to hurt others to get ahead.

Control of information and all outlets of knowledge

To keep knowledge of Light and its teachings from spreading, Dark leaders will suppress or try to gain absolute control of all forms of media (like newspapers, online news sites, and so on) as well as all educational institutions (not just colleges and universities, but even schools for young children and teenagers) so that the truth is only on the surface. Our idiot boxes (aka TV) is a highly controlled aspect, repeating the dark philosophy sugar-coated with truths over and over again with different names and different faces.

Use of technology

This is a huge topic, very briefly stated here. Humanity is in the lower rungs of consciousness so our perception of life and the universe is very limited. There are technologies by both Dark and Light that are beyond current human understanding. The beings have been in existence for millions of years compared to a few hundred years of technological advancement of the human species. AI is just one of the technology that Humans are exploring currently.

Cultivating a sheep mentality for humans

Related to this, Dark leaders will try to prevent independent thought among those they control and train their societies to follow the commands of politicians or monarchs without thinking. We are like sheep being pulled to the slaughterhouse. (The great light beings of the cosmos watch with great sadness as the humans are being taken to the slaughterhouse of their own volition).

Distortion of religious scriptures and teachings

Ensouled Humans are wired such that there is an upward gravitational pull to grow, evolve, and become closer to heaven and the source. Religion is a natural element that aids in growth. Dark beings use this as a powerful weapon. Most organized religions of today are controlled in so many ways. It is beyond the scope to discuss anything more on this.

Creating more Karma

To be discussed in future chapters, Dark entities want people to generate negative, rather than positive, karma to keep their souls trapped in this universe, so their spiritual activity creates energy for Satan's side. Thus, they will allow humans to survive but not truly flourish.

DNA manipulation

Dark politicians and scientists try to find out fragments of DNA in people that can confer enlightenment and destroy them. They have also tried to manipulate DNA in people (often without their consent) to make their servants more malleable and dull-witted. Over time, they want to alter human evolution to create as many subservient slaves as possible and have done this throughout history and continue to do so in sophisticated ways. Many people barely notice it; it is as subtle and omnipresent as the Matrix in that Morpheus and Neo fought. There are many books and movies that capture the importance of DNA for evolution. There is some level of truth in these books and or movies.

Suppressing Knowledge

This is the most important aspect of Dark plans. They want to suppress knowledge of all higher spiritual realities and destroy all evidence of humanity's past to better control us.

Influential organizations

Dark ones will create groups such as the Illuminati, subversive cults, and certain Freemason groups (though not all!) to carry out their plans. Some groups will openly declare that they support Satan's rebellion, like the "Children of Satan" or "Fallen Angels," and so on. Sometimes Dark entities in disguise will lead these organizations, while other times they are led by mere humans who are in contact with Dark entities. These groups will try to make themselves out to be harmless or even sometimes philanthropic—but they will always be dedicated, in reality, to getting their adherents into positions of power. They will try to cultivate politicians and make their own members CEOs, tech moguls, and so on. This is one way Satan tries to win the conflict while still obeying the rules of non-interference.

Keeping power/positions within families

Enough said, you get the picture.

Deceit

This is probably the most powerful weapon of Darkness in my opinion. Do you recollect any events in recent history that has taken away your liberties and freedom in the name of so-called security? Every liberty taken away from the people is a gain for the Dark agenda. Dark is extremely intelligent in how it operates. Conditions are created so that Humans willingly give away liberties and freedom. It is beyond the scope to go any further. This is your homework. Can you think of any events or situations in the world that made you give your freedom away little by little?

Astral Travel and Selling One's Soul

We have mentioned the astral level of reality previously, but it is time to analyze in more depth what lies there, how we can directly delve into those mysteries, and how to minimize the risks of doing so. Although science and so-called "modern" ways of thinking dismiss this aspect of reality, it has gained more and more attention in the past twenty years. Out-of-body experiences (OBEs), in particular, have become very notorious and you can read many news articles in a wide variety of places, both in the West and the East, attempting to explain this phenomenon. Here we will discuss several different types of OBEs and what each tells us about the struggle between Dark and Light.

Near Death Experiences

These occur when someone has suffered a very grave injury, like a heart attack or massive blood loss after a car accident, and is in the process of dying. However, before they pass away completely and irreversibly, they are rescued by doctors or medical personnel, and their lives are saved. Since they came so close to death, they still remember the sensations they had when they were passing into it from life, and these recollections are what we call Near Death Experiences, or NDEs.

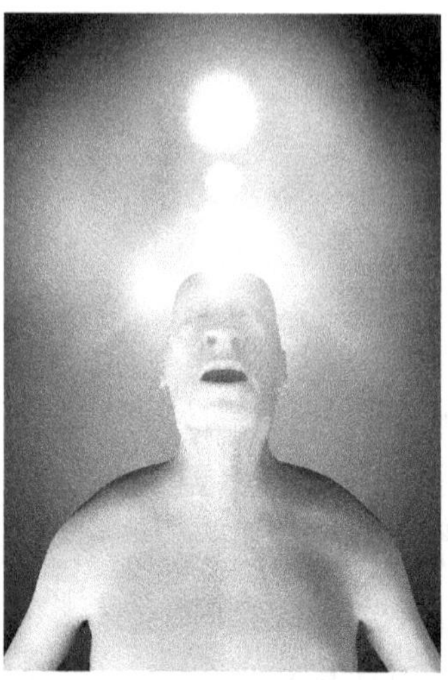

There are two kinds, positive and negative. Positive NDEs are more common. When they are near death, most people report their spirits rising up, and somehow being able to see their own bodies below them, as if they were floating–which would be impossible if the mind was only physical. They also report a sense of peace and well-being, often being drawn into a dark tunnel, the exit of which is a point of bright light they are being drawn towards. As they get closer to the light they feel more strongly the presence of God, until they are resuscitated by the doctors or medical personnel who save their lives.

Negative NDEs, on the other hand, involve the dying person feeling trapped in a state of great sadness and despair, often feeling keenly the strong absence of God, and surrounded by evil, laughing creatures and the tortured wails of many forsaken souls.

These experiences prove that there is indeed existence after death, and death involves your consciousness being released from its physical moorings and getting closer to the astral plane. The astral plane is associated with the physical one in the sense that beings from it can affect the physical level, but it might be wise to consider the astral zone an *extension* of the physical one. It is like a doorway, a place of transition, from which one can access many other higher spiritual realms of existence. A Light-aligned soul will ascend to planes closer to God, which is how positive NDEs occur. However, if a soul is Dark-aligned, or perhaps if demons are interfering, it will be dragged to planes where Satan holds sway.

LSD, Other Drugs, and Hallucinations

There are ways to access higher realities that don't involve almost dying. Specifically, many types of drugs can allow you to do this. However, to make it absolutely clear:

These methods carry extreme risks of their own, and you could die anyways if you misuse these drugs. LSD, Ayahuasca, and even milder hallucinogens like marijuana can cause brain damage, psychological problems, or addiction if overused or even used at all by certain people with certain medical conditions. Also, demons or other evil entities might be able to attack you or even possess you during astral travel using these drugs. This section is meant *only* to provide the reader with information and is absolutely not intended as an endorsement of drug use.

LSD is sometimes called acid, and it is usually found on blotter paper or as gel pills or tablets. Ingesting this substance can cause extreme hallucinations and occasionally what is called "ego dissolution." In most cases, the hallucinations are of completely random ephemera with no relation to reality in any sense, but occasionally, one can see into the astral plane, and from there spy on inhabitants of that and other planes, whether they be Light or Dark. However, those entities can occasionally notice you on those "trips" and try to contact you. Not only is it difficult to ascertain the difference between genuine spiritual communication and mere hallucinations, but it is also very hard to tell whether an angel or a malevolent demon is talking to you! The same caveats apply to Ayahuasca, which has been used by some Indigenous American shamans to access higher planes, although this substance is usually consumed as a brew rather than a pill. Experienced shamans are usually very good at navigating the higher realms safely, but someone without any knowledge or experience will be very vulnerable to evil attacks or subversion. Thus, it is a good idea to avoid drugs entirely if without the consultation of doctors and experienced priests, missionaries, or shamans.

Dreams and Visions

Finally, your consciousness can pierce the physical veil and peer into the astral realm on its own. When this occurs while you are sleeping it is called a "premonitory dream", whereas a "vision" is when this happens when you are wide awake. Even I am not entirely sure of what the requirements for each are, though premonitions in dreams are much more common.

Visions, however, are associated with lighted realms, so it stands to reason that when powerful entities, Light or Dark, want to send messages to individual humans for whatever reason, they will allow you to envision higher realities.

In the case of dreams, it may be that very spiritually attuned or psychically gifted people can free themselves of emotional or psychic baggage they deal with in their waking hours, and see higher realities that way, during deep sleep. As always, be wary of trying to learn anything in this manner, as demons can just as easily send you false and misleading messages through these media, or even accept an invitation to enter your mind. Be very careful of what happens behind closed doors. We will discuss what you can learn from dreams in greater depth in a later Chapter.

Selling of the Soul

We will not spend a great deal of time on this subject either as it is also outside the scope of this book, but to know what you are facing and to help keep you safe, you should also be aware of humans who consciously and freely choose to sell themselves to Satan.

These people can often be identified by their embrace and usage of Satanic symbols, such as pentagrams, goat's heads, skulls, and other unpleasant and unsettling imagery. Oftentimes they also even give sacrifices to stone or obsidian statues of demonic beings, such as men with the legs of goats, serpents, horned people, and so on. Deuteronomy 32:17 predicted this, as it prophesied that some "sacrificed unto devils, not to God; to gods whom they knew not, to new gods that came newly up, whom your fathers feared not."

This is not always a sure thing, as some less malevolent traditions such as Wiccanism also use five-pointed-star symbols. So, how can you tell if someone is merely dabbling in esoteric traditions or is actually worshiping Satan as divine? Most of the time, these people will not claim to be following good magics or ancient wisdom, but consciously reject Christ and God as weak and pathetic, a block to their own acquisition of power, wealth, and influence. The ways of Darkness are lucrative, and some misguided fools try to curry favor with Satan in order for a "shortcut" to attaining whatever their goals might be, and in some cases, suddenly gaining a lot of money or what seems to be good fortune seemingly overnight. These people are very shortsighted, as they do not believe in the eternity of the human soul or Heaven, and thus do not realize there are higher levels of spiritual ascendance that far outweigh all the money and power one could possibly acquire on Earth. Tragically, they do not realize that Satan doesn't care about them at all, and in the end, the only "reward" they will receive for their service to him is for their valuable, eternal soul to be corrupted and destroyed.

Dark Temples and Rituals

You might not expect people to just openly admit they serve the Darkness, but some do. There are even Satanic temples here in the United States and in other places like Europe which openly promote the worship of Satan. In many cases, these are just run by shock jocks or malcontents who don't really believe what they say and just want to scandalize the public and offend people. Some, however, are dead serious. They are run by secret societies far older and more mysterious than many of the ones you might have heard about (ex. Freemasons, Skull, and Bones). No one could even tell you the names of these scions of Darkness, such knowledge would be too difficult and dangerous to acquire even for me.

Behind the public facades of their Satanic temples, these true acolytes of Darkness perform the most fell and secret rituals to overtly invite demons or other evil spirits to attach themselves to people. These rituals involve consciously rejecting God and aligning oneself fully with evil. The participants in these rituals often become overnight sensations. By making their Dark bargains, they gain all the knowledge and expertise of a great doctor, scientist, politician, artist, or businessperson without doing any of the study or work. Thus, they gain great power, acclaim, and wealth in the physical world and in material terms. They now have the ability to bend people to their will, for the lust for dominance is (along with greed) one of the most attractive enticements Satan uses to gather minions. But, of course, these people will not find out until it is far too late that they have sold their eternal souls to the devil, and the devil always collects his due.

How to Protect Yourself and Others

Darkness cannot stand the Light, and indeed, since God rules over all of creation, is ultimately fated to lose. Even so, Satan and his minions will try to drag us down with them to Hell, and if they can't do that, they will try to make our lives hell. We have so far described the many entities (demons, evil spirits and ghosts, gremlins, etc.) and their tools (possession, physical attacks, etc.) which threaten our flourishing on Earth or our connection to God. Now it is finally time to discuss specific and actionable strategies with which we can protect ourselves *and* our loved ones against their schemes!

Methods of Self-Defense

Prayer

The Bible, both the Old and the New Testament, is absolutely chock full of stories of God answering prayers and giving those who believe in Him strength beyond their wildest dreams–physical, mental, spiritual, and emotional. So if you feel assailed by Darkness, or think you might be harried by a demon, do not waste a moment.

The first thing you should do is pray to God and Christ for deliverance. It may not be enough on its own, for only God knows the final result He is working for, and it may seem at first that some entreaties are not answered. However, it is the important first step that puts you in the right frame of mind for everything else.

Ask for Protection

In addition to prayer, folding your hands and trying to speak directly to God, just asking Him and Christ, or possibly powerful angels like Michael, to protect you can produce a good result, or at least banish lesser demons, in a short time. However, this may not work against more powerful entities.

Seek Help from Trusted Teachers, Priests, or Preachers

Everyone is at a different stage in their spiritual journey, and some of us are more advanced in the ways of Light than others. Thus, if you think you are not strong enough on your own to deal with a strong demon, there is absolutely no shame in asking for guidance or help from a religious figure you trust: A very respected priest or preacher who has demonstrated his wisdom and knowledge of religious matters, a teacher who is well versed in the spiritual, and so on. Such beacons of the Light might have the spiritual force necessary to combat the evil attacking you, or if they don't, they might know strong allies of the Light who can.

Practice Awareness

Aside from getting external help, building yourself up internally can also protect you against the Dark. Specifically, focus on becoming more spiritually aware and less concerned with material things. While you obviously shouldn't completely disregard your finances and your health and well-being, these things can distract from higher spiritual realities and the ultimate fate of your soul. Thus, concentrate on paying more attention to the world around you and be less concerned with the outward appearance of things. In this way, you can gradually perceive the spiritual aspects of seemingly mundane things and activities, and thus become more aware of the great conflict between Light and Dark that is going on all around us. And with that awareness, you can more easily avoid the many dangerous situations described previously and give our Dark enemies fewer opportunities to entrap you.

You must also become aware of yourself–that is, perhaps, the most important key to spiritual safety. By honestly and self-consciously admitting what your weaknesses are, and any wrongs you may have done to others, you can begin working on correcting those weaknesses and making up for transgressions against the people around you. In this way, you will become more and more aligned with the Light, and though demons will step up their efforts to corrupt you, the power of the Light makes you better able to resist them.

Practice Healthy Discipline and Meditation Techniques

In addition to prayer, many good and knowledgeable sages of Light also advocate for meditation. Some Christians think it can be Satanic, but that is very much untrue. There is not a single passage from the Bible that condemns meditation or asceticism, and there is absolutely no reason these practices cannot be used in conjunction with a solid prayer schedule. There are already many good books on Christian meditation so we will not delve into the subject in great depth here, but suffice it to say that taking an hour, or even half an hour, out of every day to sit peacefully in a quiet place free of distraction; breathe deeply, steadily, and evenly; close your eyes; and rid your mind of distractions can do a wonderful job of restoring your emotional balance. This means demons will not be able to exploit your emotional wreckage!

Some self-disciplinary measures, like fasting (as in the Catholic tradition) or giving up certain things on certain holidays (again, such as Lent in Catholicism) can also help calm your mind, and even better, teach you to be satisfied with what you have and unconcerned with deprivation. This will banish greed from your soul and thus banish one of the most persistent and dangerous weaknesses that demons love to latch on to.

Intuition

Sometimes your gut feeling is the best guide for avoiding Darkness. Our instincts are often more in tune with spiritual realities whereas our conscious, educated minds are too blinded by other things to see what's in front of our metaphorical nose. If you get a bad feeling from someone, or just get bad vibes from a situation or place, even if you can't explicitly describe what feels wrong, that may be your instincts telling you what darkness is about, no matter how innocuous things seem. And since demons are so good at disguising themselves and making themselves seem harmless, instinct and intuition are often the only things that can see through them. So listen to your gut feeling and your intuition always.

Energetic Protection

Finally, through the power of Jesus as well as powerful agents of Light such as angels, you can acquire day-and-night spiritual protection from Darkness. Sometimes when things are dire or there is someone the Light absolutely cannot afford to lose, higher beings actively (but subtly) intervene in the life of human beings. Unlike demons, such blessed people do not immediately gain wealth or power or fame. However, perceptive or psychic observers can tell the auras of such people are much stronger and more wholesome, with any 'cracks' in their energy signature being sealed by Light forces. The personal protection of higher beings makes it much harder for demons to latch on to someone and drain them.

Recognize Patterns in Your Dreams

Recall our discussion of dreams in the earlier Chapter, where we went over how sensitive people can sometimes catch glimpses of higher realms when they are asleep. Indeed, in many ways, a dream is a mirror of the soul! In this section, we will discuss how to interpret specific sights and occurrences you might see in dreams, and how it can help you avoid Dark schemes in your waking hours.

As you grow more and more attuned to higher realities and learn more about the threat of Darkness, you will realize that dreams are a gateway to both the astral realm and your own subconscious. Whereas less educated people will dismiss weird things they see in dreams as just illusions or random nonsense, enlightened people will realize that dreams can tell them a lot about themselves.

The primary way this occurs is by revealing the darkness within your own soul, which Satan's Dark forces will try to exploit. When you are dreaming, your Dark-aligned energies will often show up as snakes, reptiles, wolves, and often even stranger creatures in your dreams. Early on, when you are not very experienced, they might seem small, far away, and ineffectual, but as you become more and more aware of spiritual matters, your dreams will increase their intensity, sometimes to the point of becoming nightmares. In this case, the serpents and reptiles will become great leviathans or monstrous beasts. However, by facing these beasts in your dreams, or at least observing them closely, you will be able to correlate them to your unresolved emotional issues or spiritual weaknesses and work on correcting those in your waking hours.

Sometimes you will even wake up with night terrors, where it feels like someone is tormenting you. You will wake up suddenly, breathing heavily, drenched in sweat, and your bloodstream full of adrenaline, because the terrible creatures in your dream seemed like they were on the verge of eating you alive. Sometimes these are real experiences, although metaphorical ones. Those involve demons actively trying to use the astral gateway of your dreams to attack your soul itself, using the darkness in your soul, represented as serpents and creatures, as weapons.

However, in other cases, such a terrifying experience can actually be a form of spiritual training: By fighting Dark creatures in your dreams, you gradually become a stronger warrior of Light, which is why God allows such events to occur even though they can be very scary.

Now, the interpretation of dreams is a very complex topic, so we will leave it here for now and pick up the matter in a book dedicated to the subject. For now, all you need to know is that dream-journeying is very much *not* an undertaking for the faint of heart. It has many threats and there are many ways demons could use your efforts against you. Consult with experts and do as much reading and study as you can.

Personally, I have been a dreamer all my life, my way of interacting with God/Christ other than prayer, listening and intuition is by dreams. I am a big dreamer and have been a dreamer for most of my adult life. I have many volumes of scratch notebooks filled with personal dreams. Usually, I know most future potential events that affect me personally or globally when it becomes a possibility in the realms of Human consciousness or those events that God wants me to take some action. Dreams bypass the human ego doorway and it is easier for Spiritual beings to work on us or communicate with us.

Protecting Others

I'm sure many of you reading this book are not concerned only with yourselves: You also want to protect your friends and loved ones. This section will give you a few pointers on how to do so.

The first thing to keep in mind is that you can't protect others unless you have protected yourself first. So, no matter how admirably altruistic you may be (and altruism certainly is a Light-aligned trait), you need to be smart about how you go about things. Make sure you've read everything in the previous sections of this book, familiarized yourself with the types of evil entities and their weaponry, fortified your own soul and guarded yourself against demonic attacks, *and* done more reading and consulted with more holy people before trying to help others.

The second thing to keep in mind is the vast strength differentials between demons on different levels of the Dark hierarchy. Even if you are a faithful and spiritually-aware person, just saying "In the name of Christ, leave my friend alone!" will do absolutely nothing to a very strong demon, such as a baron or certainly a prince. You can invoke Christ's name all day long to such a foe, and they'll just laugh at you and give you the middle finger (metaphorically, or if they are possessing someone, perhaps literally).

God has given some people special gifts to help others. Sometimes these are powers of physical healing, such as miraculous cures of diseases or the regrowth of amputated limbs. Sometimes it is just a particular empathy and a special knack for listening to others and solving their personal problems, however great or small they may be. And in some cases, it is a particular gift for banishing demons. For some special individuals, even the most powerful demons quail before their words. These individuals can protect themselves and others very easily, and they are very valuable allies in the struggle against Darkness.

You might be one of those who possess such gifts, but they are indeed very rare. And regardless of whether or not you are gifted in that sense or not, the absolute most important factor when it comes to banishing demons and protecting others against them is to grow in your spiritual knowledge and faith in God. The more you understand the ways of Christ and Heaven, and the more you are able to teach others about them, the more powerful against demons you will become.

Without faith in God and knowledge of Christ's teachings, even the most physically and mentally fit person is helpless against weak demons, not to mention strong ones. But by reading the Bible constantly, praying as much as you can, and making sure your life and actions align with God's word as much as you can–giving to charity, being honest with other people, and placing service to others above service to self–your spiritual powers will increase vastly, and you will become stronger with the force of the Light. Though you may never be as powerful as Christ or a great archangel, obviously, by following Christ's teachings you may gain some authority to cast out demons and banish them from other people. But that is a long and arduous path, and it is not for everyone. If your primary desire is just to protect others, advising them of weaknesses in their energy field, what sorts of emotional states can lead to demonic possession, and what dangerous sorts of secret societies might actually worship Satan can at least prevent them from being attacked, even if you personally are not yet strong enough to banish demonic attackers.

Requirements to be an Exorcist

As powerful as demons are, they are neither omnipresent nor omniscient, like God. However, the difficulties followers of God face in dealing with them prove that some demons are indeed stronger than others. As Philip J. Long (2021) has noted, there was an instance in the Bible (Matthew 17:14-20 specifically) where Christ's disciples were unable to cast out a demon, but Christ himself was able to do so easily.

We must remember that the disciples were given authority to cast out demons by Christ, and they were able to cast out the evil spirits on two previous occasions. They failed on the third, described in the passage from Matthew. Thus, they came running to Christ to help understand why they failed, even though Christ had given them power. After healing the demon-possessed person, Christ responded that the disciples simply did not have enough faith.

This incident teaches us that not all possessions can be cured just by using the name of Christ or God. Some evil spirits are much stronger and require a person of strong faith. The more strongly grounded in faith a person is, the better their chances of being able to stand against the darkness. And as you can probably guess by now, the higher-ranked a demon is, the more faith and knowledge of the Light is necessary to cast them away. The demons the disciples previously banished were lower-ranked ones, while the third one they failed against was almost certainly a powerful demon in a high position in Satan's hierarchy, meaning only a servant of Light as powerful as Christ could have dealt with it, not the lower-ranked disciples, even if they were devoted to Christ on their own.

However, it is also worth mentioning that not all people of faith are called to the profession of exorcism. God has given unique gifts to some folks (it depends on one's purpose and the requirement at the specific location). Do not try to do something you are not meant for; performing exorcisms when you don't have the power to do so is extremely dangerous. There are many other ways you can serve Light and improve the world that does not involve fighting directly head-to-head against Darkness. Leave that to the experts!

In Summary, there are two requirements:

1.   The person should have deep Faith in God or Christ

2.   The person should have the gift of Spirit or a calling to be an exorcist.

CHRIST'S SECOND COMING AND THE DARK ENTITIES

As mentioned in previous chapters, despite all the misery Satan causes, and how terrifyingly powerful he and his minions seem, we know perfectly well he is allowed to exist only by God's grace. God, being all-powerful, could annihilate Satan and the Darkness with but a word. Thus, we must conclude that there is a Divine reason Satan is permitted to carry out his schemes to the extent that he is. We will discuss what those reasons might be in the next chapter. In this one, we will discuss what will happen on Earth during God's ultimate triumph: Namely, the Second Coming of Christ!

The Second Coming in the Bible

Let us first briefly discuss the literal texts which lay out the basic outline of the Second Coming. As the Book of Matthew (22:1-30) states, there will be a period of great darkness on the Earth, with wars and famines occurring all over the place, and good people (those who follow Christ, and righteous non-Christians who follow the precepts of the Light) will be harassed and persecuted all over the world. But just when things seem darkest, just when it seems Satan has destroyed all opposition and there is no hope, "the sign of the Son of Man will appear in Heaven, and then all the tribes of the earth will mourn, and they will see 'the Son of Man coming on the clouds of Heaven' with power and great glory. And He will send out His angels with a loud trumpet call, and they will gather His elect from the four winds, from one end of Heaven to the other."

The Book of Revelation (6:1-22:17) extends this description. During the End Times, Christ is described as breaking seven seals, with things on Earth becoming more and more chaotic as each seal is broken. After the sixth seal, the narrator "looked, and there was a great multitude that no one could count, from every nation, from all tribes and peoples and languages, standing before the throne and before the Lamb, robed in white, with palm branches in their hands. They cried out in a loud voice, saying, 'Salvation belongs to our God who is seated on the throne and to the Lamb!'" The elders of the faith tell him that the faithful "will hunger no more and thirst no more;" and then, when the seventh seal is broken, the angels of God will blow their trumpets, causing Satan to fall to Earth (described as the Wormwood) and all sorts of other chaos breaking out. A huge dragon will attempt to assault the forces of Light, but Christ will destroy it. At last, the armies of Light will destroy those of the Dark and a "new world" will be born and a new Jerusalem built, with Christ reigning over the remaining righteous for eternity.

Even for seasoned experts and very faithful followers of Christ, however, this allegory might be very hard to understand. In this chapter, we will explain precisely what will actually happen during the End Times and the exact ways in which God will foil Satan's plans.

Redemption

Dark entities such as demons and evil spirits who have a change of heart will be restored to their former glory in the Light and return to Heaven after a long period of repentance and reparation, of course. Remember, many demons were angels before they fell, and even evil spirits have consciousness and thus, free will and free choice. And if a being has those things, the possibility for redemption is always open. That's how great God's love and mercy are! Thus, part of God's victory, and His construction of the "New Jerusalem," involves even some of the worst demons learning the error of their ways and rejoining the side of righteousness.

Banishing the Obdurate

Some Dark entities will be redeemed, but very far from all. Some are simply so corrupt or misguided that they would never take advantage of even God's limitless mercy. They will thus stubbornly and obstinately stay set in their ways and remain loyal to Darkness in their hearts, even after Satan and his army have been thoroughly defeated.

Such evil beings have no place in the glorious, Darkness-free world Christ will build after the Second Coming. So even though God does so reluctantly (He would like nothing better than for every single being in the universe to be saved, but He cannot abrogate anyone's free will), He will have no choice but to banish all the remaining Dark-aligned entities far away from Earth. This is what the Book of Revelations meant in its description of Wormwood falling away from the heavens and the sinful and unrighteous being cast down and away. No one, not even me, knows exactly where these stubborn entities will go, but it is a place where they will never be able to hurt anyone ever again.

Mundane, "Third-Dimension" Earth Transformed

As mentioned in the introduction, Satan has interwoven Dark energies into the fabric of Earth's reality so firmly that it might seem they are one and the same. With the Second Coming, though, these energies will be transformed and replaced with Light. Thus, our daily lives on Earth, the appearance of everything around us, and even the physical world we take for granted today, will seem completely and utterly transformed. No longer will ordinary existence seem "mundane." With Satan's deceiving veil removed, even ordinary people will be able to see higher spiritual realities and their inhabitants, such as angels, completely unaided. The world in general will seem brighter, cheerier, less oppressive, and uplifting. There will be more sun, more bright colors, and more Light. The air will be clear, free of pollution (both physical and spiritual), and the waters bright and healthy.

The Righteous Entering the New Earth

This new Earth will be pretty much Heaven, given its close spiritual proximity to God's stronghold, and all righteous human beings will enter it to enjoy the fruits of their justice and righteousness.

Astral Plane Dissolved

As mentioned in an earlier chapter, the astral plane is a sort of transitory area or gateway to the higher realms from physical reality. However, with Christ's triumph, Satan and his Dark energies will no longer be able to block humans from perceiving and connecting with those higher realities.

The astral realms are a creation of Lucifer/Satan after the fall from grace. This was created to enslave Humans, it serves as a sort of prison for Humans, wherein one's soul is not allowed to move on to Heavenly realms. This realm is also related to the concept of Karma that Lucifer introduced in this prison world. This topic is too deep and sensitive. I have discussed this in detail and so much more in a prequel to this book titled "Lucifer Rebellion. Christ vs Satan – Final battle for Earth has Begun". Will have a link at the end, please check it out if you desire to know all about Lucifer, Satan, and Christ and the battle that devastated Heaven.

However, it would suffice to say that the astral realm will be cleaned off and probably might be dissolved. With this veil removed, it would become much easier for Human to Celestial communication. Naturally, this will make communicating with God and His angels much simpler.

End of Possessions, Infestations, and Hauntings

With the purge of all Dark entities from Earth, there will no longer be any demonic possessions, nor will other evil beings like malevolent ghosts, evil spirits, or the gremlins mentioned in Chapter four be able to harass and hurt human beings. Also, every location on Earth will be full of Light and there will no longer be any emotional imbalances or sites of great anger and misery, so we will no longer see any hauntings. Those entities that are trapped will be set free and be judged according to their deeds.

In other words, there won't be any scary places like abandoned hospitals or grim graveyards. Such locations will be redeemed by the Second Coming and, as hard as it may be to believe, will seem as bright and cheery as a park or garden after Christ has redeemed the entire world. Thus, we will no longer have to worry about evil beings lurking around such places, waiting to get their claws into us, and they will be perfectly safe.

Elimination of Secret Societies and Prisons of Darkness

As described in earlier sections, the world is filled with evil secret societies that advance the cause of the Dark in secret, and even many evil temples which worship Satan openly (though they might not know what they are really worshiping). Once the Second Coming occurs, all of these evil schemes and rituals will be halted entirely. With the banishing of Darkness, no one on Earth could sell their soul to the Devil even if they wanted to, and obviously, no one would want to at all after that point. Misguided people who just wanted to shock and offend will be redeemed and join the rest of us in joyfully acknowledging Christ's kingship and God's love, while the most obstinate and irredeemable humans who tried to rise (or more accurately fall) to demon-hood will be banished along with their truly demonic fellows far away from Earth, thus revealing that the ultimate reward for rejecting God is nothing but shame, humiliation, and ignominy.

Another positive result of the Second Coming is the elimination of "Dark prisons." Remember, demons can "level up," so to speak, by leaching energy from unfortunate people they have latched on to. To this end, the forces of Darkness have constructed prisons, both physical and spiritual, where they trap large numbers of people and torment them with Darkness, with the negative energy caused by corruption fueling the advancement of some demons, or the enhancement of certain Dark technologies, rituals, and weapons they use against Light. Again, in some cases, these prisons trap people's physical bodies (this is the explanation for many of the disappearances you might see in the news), or spiritual cages in the astral realm that trap the souls of those who passed on but could not evade the grasp of demonic creatures.

Fortunately, Christ will utterly smash all these prisons when He returns and destroys Satan's forces. Their inhabitants will be freed and incredibly thankful for having been liberated, and along with the rest of us, will spend the rest of their days in joy and freedom to make up for the horrible suffering they endured at Satan's hands when they were trapped. All these elements are what the vivid descriptions in the Book of Revelation are supposed to symbolize.

Conclusion

It is for this reason that the very weakest, most humble human being in the entire world is in a way more powerful, and certainly worth infinitely more, than the oldest, most esteemed, and very strongest demon, even ancient Satan himself. These creatures were given the greatest opportunities to pursue the path of Light, but to paraphrase the Old Testament, they gave up their heritage for a mess of potage. For all their fell knowledge and evil power, they are incapable of truly helping others, even other demons, and even if they were not destined to fall before Christ, all of their accomplishments would be rendered meaningless by their spite, malice, and selfishness.

Even the lowest human beggar, on the other hand, can struggle nobly against the forces of Darkness, and in doing so display more courage, strength of spirit, and compassion than these beings could ever dream of doing in a million years. And while the strongest demons are fated to be banished to ignominy and humiliation, we humans of Earth, despite the brevity of our lives and the pain of our struggles, will be seated before the throne of the Creator of the universe Himself when it is all over. With this knowledge, I can leave you, my friend, with five last pieces of advice that will help you in your journey, whether you are fated to endure a lot or a little.

Make the Best of the Time You Have

As humans, we are fated to die, and though Christ will return soon, no one knows exactly when He will come back. But either way, that doesn't change how we should live. Whether or not we die tomorrow, or whether or not Christ comes back tomorrow, in ten years, or in a hundred years, we should spend every moment we have available as well and wisely as we can. We shouldn't waste our valuable time on selfishness or vanity or petty material things, as all of that will pass away, either at the time of our death or when Christ returns and transforms the world. By spending time instead on charity, cherishing our friends and family, and making the world a better place, the limited time available to us will multiply our joy a hundredfold in the world to come. Our time on Earth is like a vapor that vanishes as dawn.

Understand the World Around You

Your challenge in this world, as is mine, is to better understand the darkness both around you and within your own soul, so you can fight it and thus evolve in spiritual maturity, growing closer to God and Christ. Always seek wisdom, read the Bible as much as you can, and regard everything and everyone around you, including yourself, with a critical and probing eye. By understanding the ways of Darkness you can fight them with the ways of Light, so mindfully make all of your actions in keeping with Christ's teachings, encourage others to do the same, and avoid those who refuse.

Recognize and Fight Against Deceit

Satan is the father of lies, and indeed, deceit is above all else how Darkness has managed to control the world for so many millennia, and why it still does so today. The demons deceive people into thinking the supernatural does not exist, they lie to people with false promises of fleeting fame and fortune.

You must learn to recognize those who have been possessed by demons, and even those who might be demons wearing the skins of people. Above all, you must always pay attention to people's deeds, not just their words. It is very easy indeed to mouth empty platitudes in the name of God or Christ or the Light. But since demons love lying so much, of course, they would be more than happy to pretend to be servants of God. But reality always comes through in actions. If someone pretending to be good does not actually do good things, whether giving to charity, acting honestly in their dealings with others, or adhering to Biblical guidelines in their daily life, they are at best a fraud, and at worst a servant of Darkness, demonic or not.

Become a Prayer Warrior!

Prayer is your number one weapon against darkness. Prayer is how we communicate with God and it shows we are grateful to Him for His endless love for us. By praying, you will find you understand the Bible better, you grow in emotional strength, and your soul becomes more attuned to the Light, strengthening you against all threats, mundane and supernatural. Even better, the more you grow in your faith, you are less easily tempted by material things, nor do Satan and his imps have an easy time deceiving and misleading you. Prayer helps keep your faith steady on the "straight and narrow" road and ensures your path leads nowhere except to Heaven.

Remember Where the Real Treasure Is

We are here today and gone tomorrow. When one passes over to the other side after death-sleep, this whole material world will soon become a dream. You do not grieve when you must change into a worn-out coat that has served its purpose. How foolish it is to think that this body (materialistic one) is permanent. It seems real now but will disappear.

One way or another, this world also will pass away. Thus, do not be concerned with money or fame or otherworldly things, for they are entirely temporary. Instead, heed Christ's words in Matthew 6:19-21: "Store up for yourselves treasures in Heaven, where moths and vermin do not destroy, and where thieves do not break in and steal. For where your treasure is, there your heart will be also."

His purpose was, above all, to fight Darkness during the Second Coming, so your best hope of achieving everlasting glory along with him is to follow His advice!

THANK YOU

I want to thank you personally for reading this book.

I have poured my Heart and Soul into these pages. I hope you have gained some valuable insights from the information presented. Please consider leaving your valuable review. Your review and feedback are important to me. Thank you so much.

Review Request – Please scan the QR code to leave your valuable review. Thank you

Lucifer Rebellion. Christ vs. Satan – Final Battle for Earth Has Begun

Multiple Award-winning Book

"extraordinary book"   "Definitely a five-star read"   - [International Review of Books]

Ever wonder **why there is a War between GOD and the Devil?** Ever wonder how the **War in Heaven started or what the Lucifer Rebellion is**?

Ever wonder why War in heaven came to Earth or why darkness still exists on Earth? And why did God send Christ to Earth?

This book explores:

- How and Why did the **war in Heaven start**? How did the War in Heaven come to Earth?

- Why did **God send Christ** to planet Earth? Was it to save Humanity and the Universe?

- What exactly happened during **Christ's First Coming** event? What is expected during the Second Coming event?

Trinity takes us on a **journey beyond time and space** to find the answers to these questions that every believer should know.

Lucifer Rebellion. Christ vs Satan – The Second Coming of Christ

Ever wonder **why there is a War between GOD and Devil?**

Ever wonder how the **War in Heaven started or what Lucifer Rebellion is?** **and why War in Heaven came to Earth** and why darkness still exists on Earth?

This book explores:

- How and Why did the **war in Heaven start**?

- How did the War in Heaven come to Earth?

- Why did **God send Christ** to planet Earth? Was it to save Humanity and the Universe?

- What are the effects of War on Earth and in Heaven?

- What exactly happened during **Christ's First Coming** event?

- What is expected during the Second Coming event?

I invite you to join me on a journey beyond space and time when the Lucifer Rebellion started and the reasons for Christ's First and Second Coming events.

Son of Man becomes Son of God. One Event that Changed the History of the World

Award-Winning Book

"an opportunity for the reader to embark on a journey with Him, feel what He feels"

"A fascinating description and story of how Christ emerged, changed and developed into the highest of holiest beings, second only to God."

"An exceptional and well-written novel without the preaching and pointless prose and verbiage of others of this type"

There is **ONE event** that is the true turning point in the history of Earth. This is not the Birth or Baptism of Jesus, but it is the **fight with the Devil**

Ever wonder what would have happened to Earth if Christ failed against Satan? This was a real possibility, although it is considered blasphemous to talk about it.

Welcome to Heaven. Your Graduation from Kindergarten Earth to Heaven

"I go and prepare a place for you, I will come back and take you to be with me that you also may be where I am." - John 14:3

Ever wonder **if Heaven is real**? What **proof** do we have?

How does one **go to Heaven**? What are the **minimum requirements for Heaven**?

Why <u>**Life of Earth is your Kindergarten school**</u>?

Trinity explores the following:

- Isn't Heaven **just a mind concept**? What is the proof of its existence? Why do I even bother about Heaven? What is in it for me?

- What are the **minimum requirements to go to Heaven or the ticket booth to Heaven?**

- Why is life on Earth your **kindergarten school**?

- Are there **different levels to heaven? If so, how many? What are they?** Does the **time and space continuum exist in Heaven?** If so how different is it compared to Earth's time and space?

Your Life in Heaven. Family, Marriage, Sex, Work

"No eye has seen, no ear has heard, and no mind has imagined what God has prepared for those who love him." – 1 Corinthians 2:9

Ever wonder what your **life in Heaven will look like after your mortal death**?

Is there **Marriage** in Heaven? Do you have a **Family in Heaven**?

Do you have your **Parents or kids or your siblings** in Heaven?

Do you have **Sexual intercourse** in Heaven?

And what do you do all day? Is there a **daily Job**? Oh. And will you meet your **deceased family members**, friends, and relatives?

These are questions that curious minds like me ask. You will find **authoritative un-speculated** answers here.

From Suffering to Healing

"I highly recommend this for anyone *who has ever suffered in their lives*, and, in all honesty, who hasn't?"

Why do **bad things happen to good people**?

Why does your **Life journey lead you to suffer?**

The Answer is to Heal You.

Your suffering is the epitome of a **blessing in disguise.** Wrapped in darkness and suffering, it removes the ground from beneath your feet and leaves you fearful, fragile, and devoid of meaning in life.

Most beings that we adore or worship have gone through dark times in their life. This includes Christ, Buddha, Gandhi, Nelson Mandela, Oprah, Abraham Lincoln, etc. This process is necessary as it redefines a person, re-makes one character, and chips away the darkness to bring out the luster of your **Real Self.** This is your **METAMORPHOSIS.**

<u>**Award-Winning Book**</u>

Our wounds are often the openings into the best and the most beautiful parts of us." -David Richo
Ever wonder **why suffering happens for no known reason...**

Ever wonder **why your Soul is longing...**

Have you ever felt like you have a **splinter in your mind, that does not let you off the hook..**

If so, <u>**you are chosen for a purpose. There is GOD's hand working in your life.**</u>

While there are many reasons people suffer (most are self-made or bad decisions or external in nature); the type of Suffering referred to as the "Dark Night
of the Soul" has a clear and definite purpose. ***The purpose is your Soul's growth.***

<u>**Your Answers and Healing await. Click on Buy Now.**</u>

What Happened on Easter Saturday? 36 hr mystery between Death and Resurrection

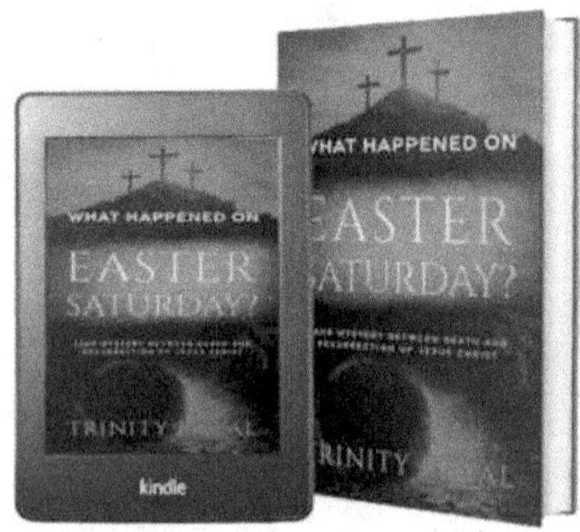

"A five-star read, absolutely."

"It stands to reason that Saturday was a critical time for Him"

"I highly recommend this incredible book as it takes the reader through both the physical and spiritual journey of Him as he underwent His transformation. **A *five-star read, absolutely*.**"

"I for one never really thought about that Saturday, so for me **it was a riveting experience**, learning about that previously overlooked time."

Ever wonder **what happened when Christ was inside the Tomb for 36 hrs** between death and resurrection?

Ever wonder **what body did Christ have after Resurrection**? and why the **resurrection process take 3 days?** why not 1-day or 2-days?

Free books to our readers

War in Heaven came to Earth. Satan Rebellion:

https://dl.bookfunnel.com/ea12ys3dmk

Your Life in Heaven:

https://dl.bookfunnel.com/vg451qpuzs

References

References

King James Bible. (2017). King James Bible Online. (Original work published 1769)

Ballard, J. (2019, October 21). *Many Americans believe ghosts and demons exist | YouGov.* Today.yougov.com.

Kashiri, T. (2023, January 11). *Who and What Are the Demons and the Angels in the Bible?* TheCollector.

Long, P. J. (2021, December 8). *Why Couldn't the Disciples Cast Out the Demon? Matthew 17:14-20.* Reading Acts.

Luke 4 NIV - - Bible Gateway. (n.d.). https://www.biblegateway.com.

Sherry, P. (2019). Problem of Evil | Definition, Responses, & Facts | Britannica. In *Encyclopædia Britannica*.

About Author

Trinity is a multi-award-winning author and a spiritual warrior. While life might not always work out according to plan, Trinity was able to take valuable lessons from each new experience. Trinity grew and developed and now shares a passion for enlightening others on spiritual knowledge in the hopes of closing the gap between Heaven and Earth. Trinity's writings reflect the depths of a passion and desire to connect with everyone seeking spiritual growth and education.

You can learn more at www.RocketshipPath2God.com or @ https://www.facebook.com/TrinityRoyalBooks